Praise for *Greater Fortune*

"The best thing about Greater Fortune is that it's written by a true inspiration to me. Marie Cosgrove knows what it's like to fail, over and over, and to get back up every time. Her book is more than just an inspiring read: it's a gift to the rest of us to be able to learn from her incredible experiences."

—Nick Vujicic, evangelist, motivational speaker, and *New York Times* bestselling author

"Marie Cosgrove embodies all the elements of a superhero. Her super powers are faith and relentlessness. She shows you the true meaning of allowing nothing or no one to stop you from living your best life. Marie's journey is one that will make you laugh, cry, appreciate the small things in life, and recognize that anything is possible when you hold on."

—Les Brown, international motivational speaker

"So many career guides make grand promises about the advice within, while glossing over the fact that we all have unique disadvantages, challenges, and hardships. What sets *Greater Fortune* apart is that Marie Cosgrove embraces these things as part of the journey, genuinely wanting to help EVERY reader succeed. In the pages of her book, you'll find the best mentor you've ever had."

—Mirela Sula, founder of *Global Woman Magazine*

"Marie Cosgrove has mapped out the path it took me years of personal and professional pain and heartache to discover for myself. With this book as my guide, much of that pain would have been avoided and my own path to success and happiness would have been much shorter."

—Barbara Allen, head writer for *American Snippets*

"*Greater Fortune* reveals the power and unwavering nature of the human spirit in its quest for survival and success. Not only is this book unputdownable but it sheds light on the journey rather than the destination, peeling back the curtain on what it means to keep going to get to where you want to be. An absolute must read for anyone navigating their own journey to success and a helpful companion to remind you that you are not alone on the path."

—Dr. Michele Di Blasi, cardiologist

"An inspiring new book, *Greater Fortune* will motivate you and set workable guidelines and goals on how to be successful in one's personal and professional life. Marie Cosgrove shares her personal experiences of fighting the odds and finding success in a male-dominated industry. Marie shares how to convert negative events in one's life into creative and productive new ideas for personal success. She has a gift in assessing 'trials and tribulations,' helping others to discover their own talents, and to redirect one into a new 'way of thinking of themself',' for their personal fulfillment and growth. Her logical analysis and approach to solving problems is exemplary. New problem-solving skills and enlightened perception of oneself is presented in a strikingly unique and powerful manner. She will help you discover true values and unique individual talents in you that has not been known by you up-to-date. Her *Greater Fortune* is not a fantasy but a well perceived, logical strategy to achieve personal happiness and success."

—William R. Martin, MD, diagnostic
and interventional radiologist

"If at times the challenges of livelihood and life overwhelm you, or if you are not sure your situation is what 'success' should look like, open this book. Marie Cosgrove knows firsthand what it's like to be born unwanted, grow up disadvantaged, be a single mom, survive an abusive marriage, and be fired. Never giving up—she turned everything around even to the point of buying the company that got rid of her. *Greater Fortune* shines a light on the path to lasting success."

—Mark Mackie, MA, JD, attorney at law for The Mackie Law Firm, PLLC and writer for RealClearPolitics

"Marie Cosgrove provides a compelling personal narrative as a demonstration of how the worst moments of one's lifetime can create the greatest foundations for personal growth—if only one chooses for it to be so. It is not trite to say that 'iron sharpens iron' but it is truly Marie's persistence that determines her success. At each crossroad, she chooses not to fail. Her choices cemented the principles in this book. They are principles anyone, in any situation and born of any circumstance, can choose to use. As one personal witness to a small part of Marie's story, she is both that irresistible force and that immovable object—born of adversity and self-made in every good sense of the word. The advice she provides is clear, hard-earned, and true."

—Andrew K. Meade, Esq, attorney at law for Meade & Neese LLP

GREATER FORTUNE

GREATER FORTUNE

**Essential Lessons from
the Entrepreneur
Who Bought the Company
That Fired Her**

MARIE COSGROVE

BenBella Books, Inc.
Dallas, Texas

BenBella Books, Inc.
10440 N. Central Expressway
Suite 800
Dallas, TX 75231
benbellabooks.com
Send feedback to feedback@benbellabooks.com

BenBella is a federally registered trademark.

Printed in the United States of America
10 9 8 7 6 5 4 3 2 1

Library of Congress Control Number: 2020949753
ISBN 9781950665389 (trade cloth)
ISBN 9781953295156 (electronic)

Copyediting by Michael Fedison
Proofreading by Kim Broderick and Amy Zarkos
Text design and composition by PerfecType, Nashville, TN
Cover design by Sarah Avinger
Cover photo © Shutterstock / Zenzen
Printed by Lake Book Manufacturing

Distributed to the trade by Two Rivers Distribution, an Ingram brand
tworiversdistribution.com

Special discounts for bulk sales are available.
Please contact bulkorders@benbellabooks.com.

This book is dedicated to those who have a sincere desire to add value to their clients through their business ventures. And to those who genuinely love their neighbor as themselves and want nothing more than to add value to friends and family, making the world a better place.

And to the memory of my grandmother Frances Longoria, who fought hard to give me a chance at life, going against every clinician who suggested otherwise.

And to the memory of my mother, Mary "Kika," Longoria, who, despite having suffered physically and mentally through a car accident and a rape, chose to birth me into this world full of adventure.

And to my children: Eddie, Genesis, Justin, Isaiah, and Lindy. Thank you for blessing me with a life in which I will never again experience a dull moment. And, most importantly, having you in my life has gifted me with a lifetime of love and laughter.

And to my beautiful granddaughters: Amity, Zuri, and Valerie. Thank you for filling me and all those around you with the gifts of Joy, Love, and Laughter.

And to my two daughters-in-law, April and Nancy. And my son-in-law, Andrew. I appreciate and love you and am thankful to have you in my life.

And most importantly, my creator, God. Thank you for giving me life and my daily bread.

CONTENTS

xv | Introduction

01 | Chapter One: A Chance at Life

19 | Chapter One Lessons and Guides

29 | Chapter Two: Know When to Walk Away

41 | Chapter Two Lessons and Guides

55 | Chapter Three: Stand Up

61 | Chapter Three Lessons and Guides

79 | Chapter Four: Jump!

89 | Chapter Four Lessons and Guides

107 | Chapter Five: Take Big, Bold, and Daring Risks

115 | Chapter Five Lessons and Guides

135 | Chapter Six: Be Better, Not Bitter

141 | Chapter Six Lessons and Guides

157 | **Chapter Seven: Expect Challenges**

165 | Chapter Seven Lessons and Guides

187 | **Chapter Eight: Change . . . Count on It**

193 | Chapter Eight Lessons and Guides

213 | **Chapter Nine: Turn Your Weakness into a Superpower**

219 | Chapter Nine Lessons and Guides

239 | **Conclusion**

241 | **Acknowledgments**

243 | **About the Author**

245 | **Notes**

INTRODUCTION

You'll never make it in this male-dominated industry. You don't have any sales experience, and the most you will be able to sell with your little girl voice is candy. So, why don't you just go home?"

Yes, I have a small, quiet voice. But then again, I'm barely five feet tall even when wearing my two-inch heels. Because I am not imposing, people—like the president of a major medical device sales company who felt okay talking to me about my "little girl voice"—tend to underestimate me.

That suits me just fine.

In fact, I've been very successful as a petite, soft-spoken woman, though you might find it amusing to learn that my nicknames have included Smalls and Tiny. My public speaking mentor, Les Brown, calls me Grasshopper. Heck, even my biology teacher in high school nicknamed me Marie the Flea, partly because of my size and also because I was so busy, I never stayed in one spot for more than a few seconds.

What the president who spoke those words to me learned that day was that behind that soft voice was a resiliency borne out of adversity and necessity. In other words, he had no idea who he was dealing with. He had no clue that his words not only failed to tamp me down, but instead fueled my desire to succeed. And I did.

Then, later in my career, while at a different company, when told I no longer had a job, even though I was the most successful salesperson on the company's team, I could have packed it in. Given up. There were moments when I almost did. **Instead, I tapped into my inner strength and turned the moment into an opportunity that eventually led to me buying that very same company.**

And that's what this book is all about: turning it around! **Taking the challenges in front of us and using them to propel us instead of defeat us!**

In these pages, you will discover how overcoming incredible hardships can actually inspire and motivate you to shine a light on your path no matter what darkness and turmoil you may be struggling with. Because, believe it or not, your powerful mind, heart, and spirit cannot be controlled or defeated when you allow the greater you to shine.

In this book, I will be sharing moments from my past . . . my failures and struggles as well as my successes. I'm not doing this to toot my own horn, but instead to show you how the tools, skill sets, and guides I've developed and included here have helped me. Let these serve as guideposts to prosperity in your own personal and professional life.

Each chapter will begin with a piece of my life story. Then I follow up with the lessons that I learned so that you can see how

I've applied what I've learned. And, of course, we explore how you, too, can turn your own difficulties into opportunities.

Here are some of the journeys we will take in this book:

- Understanding that your past circumstances, including those you were born into, do not have to determine your future or limit what you can accomplish.
- Preparing for success, building upon it, and creating a greater life.
- Preparing for failure, learning from it, and refusing to give up.
- Dealing with cutthroat competition and bias in the business world.
- Finding opportunities in challenging times.
- Accepting, adjusting, and achieving when change occurs.
- Striving for continuous growth and expanding influence.
- Controlling emotions during stressful times.
- Understanding that financial success does not guarantee personal happiness.
- Tapping into the power of faith in every aspect of life.
- Wielding perceived weaknesses and disadvantages as strengths.

The truth is that we are all small parts of this greater world, but I firmly believe that we are all capable of creating greater lives for ourselves even amidst the many challenges we face. **We can learn to see hardships, setbacks, and disappointments as opportunities for growth.** We can rise above trials, tribulations, and grievances to achieve a fulfilling and rewarding life. In fact, some of the most beautiful experiences in life result from overcoming seemingly insurmountable adversity. And yes, I believe that the worst of circumstances and events in our lives can actually make us better, stronger, more confident, and more determined and fill us with opportunities to unleash the greatness that always lies within each and every one of us.

I'm humbly sharing my story, along with my methods for overcoming obstacles and reaching success, to inspire you. I assure you that when faced with your own daunting challenges, even crushing setbacks and failures, you can rise above, succeed, and build a greater life than you'd ever dreamed possible. Through perseverance and sheer determination, I've raised four children, built successful businesses, and created a life that, while still complicated and challenging, is fulfilling and rewarding each and every day.

That's not to say I can declare victory or that everything will be perfect from here on out. I know there will be more challenges, more setbacks, and more moments of sorrow and grief. I also know that the tools I share with you in this book have helped me face challenges head-on, and I know they will add value to you, too, if you apply them when faced with obstacles.

I'm honored to share my private and personal struggles, and my successes, because my goal is to inspire you and give you strength. Whenever I've shared my life story as a speaker, many audience members have come forward to tell me that I've given them hope.

My name is Marie Longoria Cosgrove. Some may mock my voice and my height, but I know this: I was created for a greater purpose.

Your size, your age, and your circumstances are hindrances only if you allow them to plant the seeds of doubt within yourself. And I am the proof that no person and no situation can defeat us.

While I may be called "Smalls," I know this: I can stand tall for what I believe in. I can feel tall when I do more to be more, and most importantly, I can stand tall and feel tall when serving others.

And so can you.

ONE

A CHANCE AT LIFE

I was born in McAllen, Texas, in the Rio Grande Valley—located approximately four hours south of San Antonio—as south as you can get before crossing the border into Mexico.

McAllen is a place where you could put one foot on the Mexican side and the other on the USA side—and be in two countries simultaneously. When I was growing up, McAllen was a sleepy agricultural town where everyone knew your name. I spent most of my younger childhood days at my grandparents' home, where we had two window units for air-conditioning. One resided in the combined living and dining room and the second in a bedroom an uncle lived in. So, as you can imagine, our evenings were hot and muggy. We took two showers, one in the morning to cool off from the hot, hot night, and every evening to wash off our daily sweat. There are only two seasons in the Deep South—summer and spring. Although the area is known as the Rio Grande Valley, there are no mountains. The area is flat, with not even a hill in sight. It's a place where kids grow up thinking grass is tan, not green, because of how dry it is. Fortunately, my grandfather took good care of his property and watered the grass daily—so I was one of the few kids to know the true color of grass. My grandparents had a large pecan tree in front of their humble three-bedroom home, peach trees lined up alongside, with grapefruit, tangerine, and key lime trees in the back. They also had a few berry bushes, a papaya and avocado tree, and various herbs that we cooked with. Every evening, I would help my grandparents water the plants and care for the yard. Today, McAllen has grown significantly to a population of a little over 140,000 residents.

—

Our family name is Longoria. As far as I know, I am not related to the famous actress, Eva, or the Major League baseball player, Evan. Our Longorias have a darker and cloudier history, some of which resembles a telenovela version of a Shakespearean tragedy.

Before I was born, a horrible car accident severely impacted our family, especially my mother, Mary, who was known as Kika.

The accident occurred on New Year's Day, 1969. My mom was only twenty-two and single. She was riding in a car with her parents, her brother, and her sister on a ten-hour drive from McAllen to Durango, Mexico, for a family wedding.

My grandfather was at the wheel as they drove on Mexico's infamous Federal Highway 40, sections of which are known as *Espinazo del Diablo* (the Devil's Backbone). He had been traveling a long, straight stretch for many hours in the rain on a remote area west of Monterrey, when the road suddenly took a sharp turn. At that time, there were no lights on the road, and the sign that was there had been knocked down, leaving drivers with no warning of the sharp curve ahead.

Their car missed the curve, went off the road, and smashed into a tree. Both of my grandmother's legs were broken. Her son, my uncle, just two years old at the time, flew from the back seat of the car through the windshield and landed on the hood. His legs were broken, too. I was told that his face and entire body were covered in blood, and only the whites of his eyes were visible. My future mother, Kika, had the worst injuries of all. Her head was crushed, putting her in a coma. To make matters worse, it was nearly twenty-four hours before someone stopped to check on them.

And the first to do so was not a Good Samaritan. He stole all the family's belongings while they lay helpless, injured, and in agony. The next person who stopped did come to their aid. He put them all in his pickup truck and took them to the closest hospital in Torreon, Mexico.

Kika was still unconscious with blood flowing out of her mouth and head. Her sister tried in vain to stop the bleeding with her hands.

At the hospital, the ER doctor told my grandparents, "Your daughter is still alive, but she has severe bleeding in her brain. She won't live much longer."

My grandmother, a woman of unstoppable faith, told the doctor, "You must perform surgery to stop the bleeding."

"Surgery is way too risky and could result in immediate death or a permanent vegetative state," the doctor said. "Besides, we have no one on staff who can perform this operation. We would have to call in a surgeon from another city, and by the time he arrives, your daughter will be dead."

My heroic grandmother persisted. She begged and badgered the doctor until he relented and called in a surgeon who performed the difficult operation. Kika remained in a coma after the surgery. In fact, two months later, she was still on life support with a breathing tube down her throat. That's when the doctors told my grandmother that it was time to pull Kika off life support. And that she had no chance of recovery.

A few nights before, my grandmother had had a dream in which Jesus told her that Kika would live. That dream strengthened my grandmother's already strong faith, and she refused to accept the prognosis. "We want to take her to the United States for treatment," she told the doctors.

My grandmother felt specialized care in the US was the only hope, and the rest of the family accepted her decision. My uncle, Jesus Cantú, rented a van with a gurney and hired a nurse to transport Kika back to McAllen. She remained in a coma throughout the trip. At one point, her vital signs dropped alarmingly, so they had to stop in Monterrey until she was stabilized and they could continue.

Kika remained on life support for another month at the McAllen General Hospital. The doctors there kept urging my grandmother to take her off life support, saying Kika would never emerge from the coma. Finally, the hospital demanded she be taken off life support.

My grandmother pleaded for one more day and ordered everyone in the family to begin around-the-clock prayer.

The next morning, Kika opened her eyes. She tried to speak but was unable to do so until the medical staff plugged the hole doctors had made in her trachea for the breathing tube.

"Can I have a strawberry milkshake?" she whispered.

—

It took my mom more than a year to physically recover. She had to relearn how to walk and speak, but she suffered permanent brain damage that left her judgment impaired. This led to another tragic situation just a few months after her recovery.

While out for an evening with friends, she was attacked and raped. She became pregnant as a result.

Doctors told my grandmother that Kika should not have the baby. That the strong medications Kika had been on since the accident would adversely affect the child, who could end up with serious birth defects. Along with that, being mentally impaired would affect her ability to raise the child.

My grandmother was moved when Kika pleaded to keep her unborn child. "God saved my life, and I'm not going to take life away from my baby!" she said.

Again, my grandmother's faith was tested. Her faith may have bent . . . but it never broke, even knowing that shame would come with a child born of rape to an unwed mother. She decided that God had brought this child for a purpose that was beyond her understanding, and she promised to help raise the child.

The baby was born on June 5, 1970.

They named me Marie Frances Longoria.

—

There were times in my childhood and teen years when I doubted the wisdom of the decision to bring me into the world. I was shunned and treated as an outcast because I was the child of a mentally handicapped mother and an unknown rapist. Even certain family members bullied me. Sadly, they did not always treat my mom with respect due to her disabilities. I believe that they just didn't know how to connect with her, due to her inability to communicate as normal people do, and they found it easier to ignore her.

The common message I heard growing up was, "You are not part of the family. You don't have a father. You are a bastard. You are cursed. You are not a true Longoria because your dad was not a Longoria."

My schoolmates wouldn't play with me because of that stigma. I was also falsely labeled as mentally impaired because of my mother's condition. As a result, I was placed in special education classes when I began school. Later, I was moved to regular classes, but pulled out for special education English and math sessions because I was defined as "slow" and "dyslexic."

I remember kids saying, "She is crazy just like her mom; she has to go with the dummies!"

When I invited a friend to come to my house when I was about ten years old, she said, "My mom said I can't because your mom is crazy." I spent many recesses alone, watching the other kids play.

—

I lived with my mom for the first five years of my life. I was removed from her care after she went out one night and left me alone in the apartment. This was not a singular occurrence. When it happened, I would often go to a neighbor's house. I remember how nice the neighbor's older teen daughter was. She gave me cookies and spent time with me. I thought she was a princess. The day I was taken from my mom, I knocked on the neighbor's house and there was no answer. They were out. And . . . I had locked myself out of my apartment. A police officer passed by and saw me crying on the front steps. He drove me to my grandmother's. (She had me memorize her phone number and address at a very young age.)

After that, my grandmother provided most of my care. I stayed with my mother on weekends, during school vacation days, and for the summers. Even then, my time with her was limited because the damage to her brain caused schizophrenic behavior and delusions, which left her without a moral compass. Once, we were given a ride by a new neighbor to the grocery store. On the way back, she got into an argument with him, and when we were almost home, she opened the door, grabbed my hand, and we both jumped out while the car was still moving. Fortunately, he was going slowly because we were approaching the driveway.

She shrieked, "He is trying to kill us! Run!"

We ran as fast as we could into the house. I was terrified and shaking. I looked out the window and saw his car on the grass. She said, "He is so crazy, he even drove on the grass to try to run us over!" I now realize, of course, that this was one of her many episodes. The neighbor always parked on the grass, but at the time, I believed he was going to kill us.

My mother had also become highly promiscuous. She brought many men into her home when I was there. Some abused me in ways too grotesque to share.

I was very close to my stepdad, George Cholick, as he would take me swimming at the beach or at a pool and roller skating almost every weekend. I called him Dad because he did not treat me like a stepchild, but rather as his bonus child. He was there for me from the moment I was born. I did not realize the truth of how I came into the world until I started getting bullied by certain family members for not having a biological father. At the age of nine, I learned about my biological father when a lady came into my grandmother's beauty salon to tell me *she* was my grandmother. I did not understand the concept of rape at that time, but that day I learned that George was not my biological dad. I also learned why I did not have the deep sky-blue eyes he had. Regardless, my love for him was not shaken in the least.

George played in a popular southern Texas band, the Country Roland Band, and boy, he could sing and play just about any instrument from the banjo to the steel guitar. He took me to private parties where his music transported me into a whole 'nother world of perfect harmony. Dad taught me to enjoy the beauty in life and to never give up on my dreams.

His goal in life was to release a record. He would paraphrase the book of Habakkuk in the Bible:

> The vision still has its time,
> Presses on to fulfillment,
> And it will not disappoint;
> If it delays, wait for it, it will
> Surely come.

He later achieved his goal and released an album with the Country Roland Band! But what Dad did not prepare me for was the suffering that is very real in this world—in this instance, his own.

One day, during the summer of my ninth-grade year, my grandparents drove me to George's apartment. I was excited at the prospect of spending the weekend with him. As we pulled up, I saw police cars and an ambulance in front of his building. My heart was racing. I ran inside, as the police surged to hold me back, but they were too late. I ran past the yellow barrier tape only to see George, my dad, hanging from the ceiling.

This was one of the darkest days. I was devastated and confused. My heart felt the deepest pain I had ever experienced to that point in my life. I blamed myself, which threw me into total despair.

No matter who my grandmother took me to, and no matter what drugs they prescribed for me, I couldn't let go of that pain in my heart—so much so that I simply could not function at school. The school counselor suggested removing me from school that year and keeping me home. And that's what ended up happening. An aunt and uncle took me in at this time, and I went to work with them every day. They would not allow me to wallow in sadness. If they saw that I had the least bit of hurt on my face, they told me to get over it. It was not that easy. My role model had given up, and I didn't know how to deal with my emotions.

I never did come to understand why my dad quit on life. Perhaps he suffered from depression due the cheating ways of my mom. Whatever the reason, I would never know.

As my memories of my dad were deeply settled in my heart and mind, I would rehash his words to me: "the vision still has its time." Eventually, I took his lessons to heart and learned from him that I needed a vision for my life. I needed to realize the power of holding onto my vision—not just holding onto a goal that ends once reached.

My hope is that my story of overcoming a series of tragedies will become part of someone's lesson on how they can not only survive but triumph through life's tough times. The one thing

I want *you* to remember is the difference between a goal and a vision. **A goal is something you complete, while a vision is something that completes you.** What is your life's vision? Hold onto YOUR vision, because your vision "still has its time."

———

I reached my teen years with little hope and few expectations for my life. I felt worthless and destined to fail.

My high school counselors told me I was not smart enough to take college preparatory courses. Instead, they steered me into basic home economics and trade courses. In fact, I was demoted from algebra class to FOM (fundamentals of mathematics), but along the way, I managed to enroll in a computer programming class. To everyone's surprise, I was good at it. I picked up the basics quickly and landed a part-time position in a local print shop.

During that job interview, they asked me if I could do programming that was more advanced than what I had learned in class. I lied and said yes.

The boss wanted to test me, so I asked if they would let me see the codes they used (Pascal, SMGL, and XML). The programmer was overwhelmed with work, and badly needed help, so she had no problem letting me take a sneak peek. In fact, she said, "Please—anything I could do to help you get this job!"

I copied the codes, took them home, and memorized them. The next day, I passed the test. The print shop gave me a full-time position after I graduated. It was during this time that I married my high school boyfriend. I was eighteen years old.

In that first full-time job, I worked on cool projects, creating brochures, programs, manuals, and magazines for clients that included the Miss USA Pageant and Maytag. I designed the graphics and did so well that the boss promoted me to marketing and sales, which included meeting with clients. Jealous of my new position and the freedom it bought me, my husband started coming to the office and following me to client meetings. He thought I was having an affair.

To placate him, I let him sit in on my meetings. I told clients he was my associate in training. Ultimately, I had to give my two weeks' notice because I knew I could not do my job under those circumstances. My boss did not want me to leave, but I could not handle the stress or the embarrassment.

Within two weeks, I found another job with a local bank. After a few months there, I was promoted to marketing manager for the main branch, and I worked there for just over three years until it was purchased by a larger bank.

During that period, my husband again grew jealous and increasingly violent. He began beating me. One day, my boss saw that I had a black eye and called me in. My boss was a Christian who possessed an incredible amount of faith. At first, he urged me to stay in the marriage. Eventually, though, my husband became so violent that I had to get a protective order. After that, the bank installed an alarm button under my desk, and my boss gave me money to file for divorce so that my children and I could escape that violent and dangerous relationship.

Soon after the divorce was finalized, I gave birth to my third child. I was twenty-five years old, and once again, my personal life was a mess and a drag on my successful work life. Yet, when the bank fired their advertising agency, they gave me all the responsibility for print and television advertising because they liked the work I did.

So, yes, my career choices had been much better than my relationship choices. I had far more confidence in my business skills than in my value as a person. My childhood insecurities lingered into adulthood. I felt unworthy, and my husband had preyed on that. He told me no one would want me, and, sadly, I believed him.

Over time and through experience, **I would learn that we all have value and we are not "orphaned."** I am a child of God, and my past, what others say about me, and what others have done to try to strip my soul from me do not matter. Because I know who I belong to, and no person can take away my soul and strip me from my faith. It is through His grace that I am here today. As stated in Philippians 4:13, "I can do all things through Christ, who strengthens me." And I am living proof.

⁓

At the bank, we made humorous in-house commercials that helped the bank grow from one location to seven in the Rio Grande Valley area. Unfortunately, that growth attracted a buy-out offer from a larger bank and put me out of a job when a new boss took credit for all my work. Instead of focusing on the unfairness of the situation, I concentrated on helping local small businesses, politicians, and nonprofits create brand awareness, revenue-generating ads, new programs, and time-saving systems. I enjoyed quite a bit of success over the next four years.

One of my clients was an orthopedic surgeon who marketed to older people suffering from bone loss. He had been advertising at peak night hours, which was very expensive. I cut his budget in half after advising him that older people were not watching television that late.

His phone rang off the hook with the new time slots and ads I created. I negotiated a commission based on the calls that came to an 800 number I set up for him instead of getting paid by project. This provided a risk-free option for him while allowing me to maximize my income.

—

Just as I was hitting my stride as a freelancer, a local banker who went to my church began expressing an interest in me. I felt no attraction toward him.

My family and friends pressured me to go out with him. Even with all my business success, I had no self-confidence socially. The guy said he was a Christian. He was active in the church and community and was well regarded. So, even though I saw some early warning signs based on what I knew about his previous relationships, I relented and began dating him.

I especially remember my aunt and uncle inviting him to Bible study at their home. During one gathering, my aunt told me that God intended for children to have a mom and a dad, and since my children's dad had lost parental rights, they needed this man as a father figure. She told me I was being selfish by not wanting to marry him. And it may have seemed selfish on my part, because this man was very generous. He provided us with amazing gifts, and from outside appearances, he seemed to possess great character. I was told I was not listening to God's voice and accepting the gift He was sending me by presenting a good man with a good job who would be a great parent to my three children. Sadly, my self-worth and self-esteem had been so beaten out of me, I did not have the strength to listen to my inner voice, so I married him. I would painfully learn that **experience occurs after**, **not before**, **you need it, and that listening to one's inner voice is essential**.

Henry David Thoreau wrote, "Public opinion is a weak tyrant compared with our own private opinion. What a man thinks of himself, that it is which determines, or rather, indicates his fate."

My situation illustrated a classic case of settling for a guy . . . the wrong guy. He sensed my apprehensions about him.

On our wedding night, he said, "I know you don't like me, but you will learn to love me."

I never did, but I stayed in the marriage despite all my misgivings. I blame myself for not having the strength to say no. I thought my children needed a father, but he turned out to be a predator.

We had been married for a couple of years when I was offered a marketing position at the San Antonio headquarters of a large insurance and financial services corporation. This was a great opportunity that included a six-figure salary, health insurance, and other terrific benefits.

They typically only hired people with college degrees, but the president of my division was impressed with my real-world experience. He said the company would pay for my education while I worked.

Even though my marriage was struggling, my husband was supportive. He offered to transfer to a bank in San Antonio. We were having issues because he was insanely strict with the kids and verbally abusive to me. A church member even told me that something did not seem right because when the kids were alone with my husband, "they are like little robots." The kids told me secretly that he hit them. I confronted him, but he denied it, saying they did not like that he made them follow his rules so they made up those allegations. I asked the kids again. They had been so manipulated by their stepdad, they admitted they had made it up. Later, we found out through counseling that he would threaten to kill the dog or hurt one of their siblings if they told the truth. Sadly, it was hard for me to see the signs at the time due to my long hours at work. I would leave the office very late, while he would be at home with the children.

So, we moved to San Antonio, where I took on the biggest job of my life up to that point. I worked with major vendors like

Fed Ex and cruise lines to supply discounts to members. The customer catalog I helped design and produce operated with a $15 million budget.

Within a year, I was promoted to marketing manager, in charge of direct mail marketing for a number of large clients, as well as developing new member products. I worked closely with our call center staff in sales techniques, and I collaborated with other departments to rewrite the scripts we used to close sales.

We became so successful, we nearly buried ourselves. I learned firsthand that if you are not prepared for success, it can overwhelm or even destroy you. This was especially true with a couple of our marketing offerings. One was an insurance card that covered all the inner workings of household appliances, and the other was a health savings card that provided discounts on prescriptions and over-the-counter medications.

The response for those two items was so strong that our phone center could not deal with all the calls to sign up. When the phone lines were tied up, customers called our other lines, which made those divisions unhappy. In fact, ultimately, we had to discontinue those products because we were unable to expand our phone centers fast enough to handle the demand. Additionally, we didn't expect the influx of sales, and we realized we were not logistically prepared to fulfill the orders, even if and when we resolved the call center situation.

We succeeded in other areas. I stepped in with a security service giant, which was not experiencing any success through our partnership. They were marketing to younger parents with babies. They ran beautiful ads, but they were not working.

I suggested that we run a test, targeting all audiences. After the test results, I recommended that they change their target market to older people who were more concerned about security for their valuables and had more disposable income than younger couples. Initially, upper management thought it was a crazy idea. After encouraging them to conduct a test to prove my theory, they agreed. Our test results proved this to be true. Within six months of changing their target market, the account was churning $2 million in profits.

My bosses began putting me in charge of other big accounts. I negotiated my bonuses based on improving performance with those accounts, and my income grew substantially.

Once again, however, my personal life was floundering as my career thrived.

CHAPTER ONE
LESSONS AND GUIDES

#1

THOUGHTS ABOUT PAST EXPERIENCES

Your past does not determine your future. Regardless of what lies behind you, greater fortune can be waiting ahead. Life's challenges, struggles, and pain should not restrict your ability and determination to flourish, to serve, and to benefit others by wielding your talents, your knowledge, your strengths, and your gifts to a waiting world. Nothing that has happened to you in the past can hold you back if you stay focused on being your greater self, tapping all of the best within and around you. According to C.G. Jung, **"I am not what happened to me. I am what I choose to become."**

1. **What happened to you in the past does not determine your future. YOU are the force for change in your life.**

   Refuse to allow the past to hold you captive as you move forward. The past offers lessons, not a life sentence. Environment, circumstances, or other elements of life may be viewed as obstacles or advantages. The choice rests with you. No government, no agency, no person, no authoritarian can oppress or free you to the degree that your own inner self can enslave or free you. **You truly do have the power within that no person, situation, institution, or government can claim without your permission.**

2. **You are fully equipped and able to rise above and beyond your formative years or overcome any adversity or tragedy that may have occurred in your life.**

   Seek help as you need it from your faith, a counselor, a therapist, or a trusted adviser . . . and know this: **you are no longer that child hoping to survive.** You have developed skills and talents as an adult that can help you not just to cope with the memories, but to transcend them.

#2

WHEN IT'S TIME TO SEEK HELP

Life is full of obstacles, challenges, and difficulties. Regardless of your age, gender, or culture, you may at times face challenges that seem insurmountable. Those challenges may come in the form of emotional pain, bad relationships, poor health, or loss of work.

Please know that whatever you are facing, you are strong enough to handle the challenge. I used my faith to help me get through major obstacles. I relied on my faith in God to give me the strength to overcome because He is bigger than any challenge that may come my way. I learned to pray, seek His wisdom, leave my problems on His shoulders, and trust in Him. As I look back at my life, I am constantly reminded of how God can turn the evil you experience, which, at times, may feel as dark as death, into new life, restoring you to a living miracle. What was meant for evil will be reversed.

I wish my stepdad had asked for help. It was there, but he didn't know how to ask for it. If you are facing struggles you feel you cannot handle alone, please seek help by:

1. **Seeking Professional Counseling**
   This is imperative, especially if you feel that you are facing emotional and physical traumas that you cannot handle on your own. You may require the assistance of trained professionals and undivided attention. And, if you are at risk of harming yourself, contact the Suicide Hotline, 1-800-273-8255.

2. **Confiding in a Friend**
   A true friend will be there to offer you moral support. A good way to identify a true friend is if they possess the following qualities:
   Are they loyal? Have they kept previous conversations you have had with them confidential? How do they treat other friends they have? Do they talk with you about

confidential conversations they have had with other people? If so, that may be a clear sign that they won't be able to keep your confidential information between the two of you. Have they provided support to you in the past and been there for you throughout your friendship?

Are they good listeners? If they tend to change the conversation and make it about them, it may be that they are too self-absorbed in their own life to be supportive. Do they place their full attention on you, putting away their phone, so they can fully listen to you?

Can the person sympathize with you? Sometimes someone will immediately try to be "fair" and instead of sympathizing with you, they immediately seek excuses as to why you are facing hardship. During difficulties, this could make the situation worse. You are already facing trouble—additional guilt placed on you, such as, "Well, maybe the other person had a reason to . . ." and attempting to play devil's advocate, may be a sign that you need to find someone else who can truly listen.

3. **Finding an Accountability Partner**

Choose someone who will hold you accountable and call you daily or weekly to check on you. A good accountability partner will help you gauge your goals to ensure that you are on the right track, helping you see potential pitfalls. Particularly in difficult times, you may not see dangers, but an accountability partner will help you identify decisions you may be making out of emotional distress that could actually take you two steps back. Your accountability partner will challenge you to push through failures, helping you to come out of them stronger and more resilient, while also helping you to achieve ultimate success.

4. **Considering a Life Coach**

A life coach can provide tremendous guidance to help you survive and overcome the challenges you are facing. A good life coach will help you find the answers to your concerns that are within you already, but you may be too overwhelmed with your situation to uncover those answers alone. Often, when we face great obstacles in business or in our personal lives, we allow our fear to control our decision making and guide our direction—or lack of direction, which can lead us further into despair. A life coach will help you see beyond those obstacles, guiding you from your perceived darkness into the light you have within you and toward the success you may not see as possible.

5. **Relying on Your Faith**

If you are a person of faith, join a study group and/or confide in your place of worship's leadership team.

6. **Seeking a Mentor**

Choose someone who has experienced similar challenges and overcome them. They will be able to provide practical advice acquired from their real-life experiences that can help you with your situation.

7. **Serving Others**

Help out others who are going through difficulties. This is probably the most healing experience you will ever encounter. When you seek ways to help others, your problems may suddenly seem less important.

#3

RESULTS TAKE WORK

Sometimes you need to expend extra effort to arrive at the results you want, and work takes time and sweat! Life is not like a microwave with instantaneous results. In fact, I've found it's more like a crockpot. If you want a flavorful meal, you must be patient and wait for it. When my grandma was expecting results for my mom's healing, she had to put in the effort to coordinate transport, procure the services of a nurse, and acquire the equipment needed to move my mom to the hospital in Texas. She prayed like her life depended on it, and she made the effort as if it all depended on her!

#4

NEVER UNDERESTIMATE
THE POWER OF FAITH

My grandmother's faith has always been a guiding principle for me. Through her powerful belief system, she saw life's challenges as temporary situations, like storms that pass, leaving only the calm behind. Faith will help you see the storms for what they are . . . fierce, but temporary.

Here are a few things I learned from watching my grandmother:

1. **Faith Doesn't Snap Under Pressure**

   Like the palm tree, which can bend up to fifty degrees without snapping during a strong storm, my grandmother's faith was just as strong during life's most difficult moments. During hardships, we tend to funnel our energy into the negative. Faith calls us to put 100 percent of our heart and spirit on future abundance waiting for us on the other side, ready to replenish our souls. My experience in healthcare has taught me about the power and resiliency of our minds. You can completely lose your mind, or instead, focus on replenishing your spirit on hope not yet seen, but with an expectant heart—knowing that this, too, shall pass.

   Studies have shown that replacing fear with faith helps you to identify solutions to your dilemma or crisis. Faith creates a calm in your spirit, whereas fear causes your heart rate to go up, increasing hormones that produce a desire to run from your problems rather than face them head-on. Fear may be necessary when you are being chased by a dangerous bear, because you need those hormones to help you run fast. However, they are not needed when you are not being chased. Your mind needs to be calm and levelheaded to think of solutions. Having a strong foundational faith will help you to identify solutions and see the brighter side waiting for you.

2. **Where You Plant Your Roots Matters**

   Just as the palm tree relies on a strong root system that prevents it from being uprooted during a storm, maintaining a strong faith during life's challenges can keep you from being emotionally or physically toppled. When you plant your faith system's roots in solid ground, no matter how difficult the situation, you can overcome any storm that comes your way.

3. **Great Things Can Happen If You Imagine with All Your Mind and Believe with All Your Heart**

   Leading cardiologist Mitchell Krucoff of Duke University found in a pilot study that, out of five randomized groups of heart patients, those who received prayer therapy had "a little more than 50 percent overall reduction" in complications. "Dr. Krucoff states that intercessory prayer has also shown promising results in studies with HIV patients and infertile couples."[1] Studies have also been conducted with cancer patients showing significant improvements of well-being.[2]

#5

THE DARKEST MOMENTS REVEAL OPPORTUNITY

It is often when it appears as though all is going against us that the biggest opportunities arise. We just need to remember not to lose hope when things don't go our way and learn to seek those opportunities. They are usually right in front of us. Focusing on our adversities clouds our thinking, and we are in danger of becoming bitter, angry, hurt, and resentful with thoughts of, "Life is not fair!" It's true—life is not fair. But that is why we need to uncloud our minds and focus on how our difficulties can, instead, propel us toward new opportunities and success!

TWO

KNOW WHEN
TO WALK AWAY

While working at my job in San Antonio, my boss had given a four-week notice that she was leaving to start her own business. A coworker wanted the position. He was also envious of anyone who had received recognition in the past and did everything he could to demean their achievements. For example, I had just increased return-on-investment (ROI) for my line of business by 56 percent within six months. Instead of congratulating me, the jealous coworker said it was purely luck that I had achieved the growth I had for my department. He responded this way to other employees as well, and since my boss was leaving, she didn't address the situation.

My coworker wanted to rise to the top, but he did it by demeaning others in order to lift himself up.

Unfortunately, this negatively affected the company and demoralized the team. Many managers quit and left, either just before or immediately after my boss moved on.

We had a very important meeting out of town, and since my boss was leaving, she wanted everyone to attend. This would ensure that whoever took over her position would be aware of operations in every department she managed. This meant that I had to attend meetings for other departments and vice versa.

We had a travel department that handled all our reservations. Back in those days, we received a written itinerary and printed tickets prior to travel. I received my tickets and had everything ready to go. My flight was at noon. Therefore, I went to the office in the morning, got some work done, and left the office, driving directly to the airport. When I arrived at the ticket counter to check in my bag, the airline rep said, "You don't have a flight today." I thought that perhaps the travel department made a mistake on my tickets, so as she handed my ticket back to me, I looked at the date and everything was correct. I told her, "Ma'am, there must be some mistake. Look, it's today's date printed on the ticket with the correct time." She said, "No, it is not popping up on my system. You are not scheduled on a flight today." I called the office and spoke to the travel department. They said, "Someone cancelled your flight. They said you didn't need to be at the meeting after all."

I called my boss, whose flight was a little later than mine; she had not left the office yet. She said, "No, you have to be at the meeting. You are presenting, and it is very important you show up!" We didn't know who had cancelled the flight, as the person who cancelled it didn't provide a name. I managed to get a flight out that same day, but I missed the afternoon session.

It turned out that my coworker was hoping I did not get to the meeting so that he could present my information as his own. He felt this would increase his chances of getting a promotion.

He also confessed that he was jealous of me because I was constantly exceeding my quota and increasing ROI. Instead of being delighted and trying to find out how I was able to achieve a high ROI, he tried to sabotage me, and while doing so, lost integrity, loyalty, and respect.

Because my boss did not address this situation or others that affected the department, every manager left the company. But that wasn't what led to my leaving this otherwise great job.

⌒

"Don't run away. Face your problems and work through them. Facing your problems makes you stronger."

That's some great advice; however, sometimes the opposite is true, and running away may actually strengthen you.

Experience (literally gained through hard knocks) has taught me that the song lyrics "Know when to walk away and know when to run" can apply to survival (business and personal) as well as gambling. And after five years at the job in San Antonio, I knew I had to walk away not only from my current personal life, but also from my professional one. My choices cost my children and me financially at the beginning, but through faith, perseverance, and setting my sights on a higher prize, my walking away turned into a journey of self-discovery and success.

———

So, there I was, in my late twenties, living in San Antonio, with four small children and my second husband. And though I lacked a college degree, I had risen to a high-paying position, managing a $600 million annual marketing budget. Life was good on the outside. But, deep down, something was wrong.

One day, I came home a day early from a business trip. I had not called to tell my husband and children of my change in schedule, so they were not expecting me.

As I walked in the front door and past the hall into the living room, I saw three of my children lined up on the floor on their knees. They were crying. My husband was standing over them, holding a belt with the metal buckle dangling at the end.

"What's going on?" I demanded.

My husband said, "I didn't hit them, I swear! I was just trying to scare them with the belt. They are crying for attention."

My husband apologized profusely, pleading that he would never, ever hurt the kids . . . that he loved them. I knew he was lying. I pretended that all was okay in order to placate him, hoping he would soon leave for work. He begged me to stay, and as he left for work, he took the minivan keys with him.

As soon as he was gone, I called my aunt and uncle—the same aunt and uncle who took me in after my stepdad died—to come and rescue us. My uncle set a land speed record from McAllen to San Antonio. I gathered the kids, gave them their suitcases and a few trash bags, telling them to pack as much as they possibly could. I didn't have time to properly pack, and we didn't have enough suitcases to fit all our belongings.

As soon as my uncle arrived, we piled into his vehicle. He didn't have space for me, all the kids, and all the suitcases. We had to empty the suitcases and put the clothes in trash bags as they were easier to manipulate to fit in the small trunk of his car. We had to leave many belongings behind. My uncle drove as fast as he could back to McAllen.

When we arrived, my uncle said, "You can't stay here. It's not safe. This is the first place he will come looking for you, and we can't hide all of you."

He dropped us off at his sister's house in a nearby town. She had recently moved into a new home, and my husband did not know where it was. However, we could only stay for three weeks because my aunt's immediate family had plans for a friend to move in with them while the friend finished her doctorate degree.

I was now three hours away from my job, and there was no way I was going back to San Antonio. I didn't have family, or any type of support, in San Antonio. Staying there meant living on the streets or going back home—where *he* was, putting our lives in danger. Leaving a secure job with insurance and great benefits may sound foolish. But the safety, health, and life of my children were more important to me than anything money could buy. I knew I was leaving all of my material possessions behind. Everything I had worked so hard for—a job that provided insurance to take care of the needs of my son with JDMS (an autoimmune disease that caused him severe arthritis and attacked his internal organs). As crazy as it sounds, it would have been much crazier not to protect the life of my children. It was going to be hard. No car. No home. No job. No benefits. But we had each other. When you are faced with the threat of harm to you or your children, you realize what's important. At that moment, you realize there is no material possession more valuable than life.

After I was able to get a protective order and knew my husband would no longer come looking for me, we went back to my aunt and uncle's house. It was a full house, as my cousin had just gotten married and was staying there until her home was ready for them to move in. We all had to sleep on the living room floor. I had no idea what the future would bring.

—

My divorce took many years and consumed all my savings. Texas is a community property state, and my spouse knew how to play the system. I pretty much lost all of my material possessions, but the most important thing was that I was awarded a permanent restraining order from my ex-husband and full custody of my children, which meant he lost parental rights and we gained our safety.

I was thankful we were now safe, but I still faced challenges. My son's illness was growing progressively worse, as not only was his joint pain becoming unbearable, but he also had asthma, skin rashes, and calcium deposits that required surgery to remove, as well as organ failure. I also discovered that my daughter had been sexually abused. She would get up in the middle of the night screaming from night terrors caused by post-traumatic stress disorder (PTSD) from the abuse she had experienced. My kids were traumatized and needed specialized therapy.

I was twenty-nine years old, a single mom with four children under the age of eight, and no steady job. I cried a lot at first, as the pain I felt in my spirit was so strong. I felt as though the darkness was caving in and there was no way out. I hoped it was all a bad nightmare, and that I would wake up from the depths of darkness. But each new day only reminded me of the darkness that surrounded me because I was not able to see the light. My heart hurt for the suffering my kids went through, and I felt as though my heartbeat fell out right under my feet. I think it is the worst pain you can experience—seeing your children suffer and having their innocence stripped away from them. I felt so much guilt for having married an abuser.

The despair was hard to shake. I cried even when things slowly became better for us. I cried and prayed in the shower and the car so the children wouldn't hear me. I cried out, asking God, "Why? Why did my children have to go through this?" "Why didn't I leave sooner?" "Why didn't You stop me from marrying this evil man?" "Why didn't You strike him down, before he could hurt my children?"

The reality is that we all have free will, and we cannot control other people's actions. We cannot control how others choose to live their lives. Sometimes people do evil things that affect innocent bystanders who may inadvertently stand in their way. Sure, God could potentially stop us before we take action. To take away our breath. To take away our life. But then we would not have free will. We would merely be mindless beings with no ability to make our own decisions to freely choose good or evil.

———

One morning, after I dropped the children off at school, I came home and opened my prayer journal, which I had not touched since the day I'd left San Antonio. I reread an old entry in which I asked God to reveal to me truth and anything that could possibly hurt my family that I may not be aware of. I realized at that moment that **my prayer had been answered**. Had I arrived home a day later, when I was supposed to, my ex-husband may have intimidated the children from telling me what happened. I may not have become aware of the situation. The injuries to my children were hidden under their clothes, so I would not have seen them so easily. I believe God opened the door for me to come home early that day.

I rediscovered Proverbs 4:23 in the Bible, which says that out of your heart is your life source. What is being spewed out of your heart is what contributes to what you are experiencing in life. This verse taught me that, although I had walked away, I still needed to apply strategies for how to experience a positive, happy, and fulfilled life source. I was full of hurt, pain, and anguish over my situation, and I desperately wanted life to flow back through me.

———

Caring for my kids and taking them to their therapists and doctors was almost a full-time job. Still, I needed to make money so we could get our own place and afford health insurance. I strung together several freelance jobs to pay the bills. One of them involved taking government records for state agencies and digitizing them to be in line with new government regulations that had just been implemented. All government agencies faced a deadline to have their documents in an electronic format in order to eliminate hard copies.

When I tried to get a contract within my state, a government bureaucrat there told me that the only way to get it was to give him 50 percent of the deal, and that if I did not agree, I would not be able to do business anywhere within the state. I explained that I had no desire to go to prison, and that I didn't look good in orange jumpsuits. I had to seek work outside of my state. I ended up winning a contract to digitize all the personal property tax filings for the state of Missouri.

But that wasn't going to cover all my expenses. Although my contracts paid well, the work was sporadic. I didn't have the capital to grow as I needed to, nor the resources to hire enough staff to assist. Most of the money went toward healthcare costs for my children, and what was left over was used for the up-front costs of equipment needed to fulfill the contract work I was awarded. So, I thought a sales commission job might offer the flexibility and income I needed. A doctor friend connected me to a medical equipment salesman who was looking for someone to take over part of his territory. The salesman worked for a distribution and sales company contracted to sell a high-end device for physicians at $35,000 per unit. The commissions were substantial. Basically, this company was contracted to serve as the sales department of various medical device manufacturers. They represented several manufacturers and a variety of devices used by doctors, clinics, and hospitals.

I talked to the salesman, who was skeptical that I could handle the position because I had no experience. I convinced him to set up a telephone meeting with the company president. During our teleconference, I explained that I had worked with huge corporate clients in my previous marketing position, and that a big part of my responsibility was to convince the executive board how to spend the $600 million budget I oversaw. I made the case that pitching my marketing and budgeting ideas was actually sales.

He was not impressed. I challenged him to give me a thirty-day trial after I paid my own training expenses. Yes, I was desperate to a point, but I had also developed a great deal of confidence in my abilities to thrive in almost any business environment. And yes, I could have despaired over my failings as a parent, and my extremely questionable choices in spouses, but I had no more time for despair or self-pity. The president said okay, and if I passed the training, I would have an opportunity for the job.

My grandmother agreed to help watch my kids while I traveled to Dallas. As promised, I paid my own expenses for the intensive three-day training course in medical terminology, enabling me to be able to explain to clinicians how the equipment helped patients reduce pain, edema, and other conditions and improve patient outcomes. I also had to understand how the equipment worked, the science behind the technology, why the technology led to improved patient care while reducing healthcare costs, and how to sell both the concept and the equipment to clinicians.

I was excited because I wanted to be more than just a consumer in society; I wanted to be a contributor. This was a great way of helping to advance healthcare by providing clinicians with solutions for better patient care and helping patients, indirectly, at the same time. This gave me the enthusiasm to learn as much as I could. At the end of the training, I scored 100 percent on all the tests. Not bad for a full-time mom of four without a college degree, I thought.

Although some sales representatives had college degrees, they were sent home because they did not pass the training. I was confident I would be offered a position with the company, until the president walked in front of the room and attempted to use his six-foot-two-inch stature as a tower of intimidation. He stated what a tough job selling this equipment was and how some candidates were being sent home because they failed the test. In addition, despite passing the test, some would not make the cut because the sales position required specific talent, above and beyond product knowledge. He said all of this while looking directly at me.

While continuing to focus his gaze on me, in front of a room of about forty males, he said, "Some in here will never make it in this male-dominated industry."

I was the only woman in the room, leaving little doubt he was referring to me.

He then proceeded to walk toward the back of the room where I was, and I said, "You were talking to me while you were up there, weren't you?"

He said, "Yes. You don't have any sales experience, and the most you will be able to sell with your little girl voice is candy—so, why don't you just go home?"

CHAPTER TWO
LESSONS AND GUIDES

#1

JEALOUSY IN THE WORKPLACE

Jealousy, that green-eyed monster of emotions, has been labeled as capable of committing "more crimes than greed and ambition together." Jealousy unchecked destroys businesses, careers, relationships, and individuals.

Jealousy reveals an individual's dissatisfaction with oneself. By turning inward, one may discover the true source of this dissatisfaction. Through contemplation, self-examination, and corrective measures, an individual can experience the phrase "Physician, heal thyself." Too often, though, jealousy is turned outward with a vengeance, leading to catastrophic results.

Perhaps you have had to face a situation where someone is envious of you. You were recognized for a job well done in the workplace, and you sensed jealousy from a coworker who felt that *they* deserved the recognition.

When someone has received an award or recognition you think you should have received yourself, you may develop a sense of anger, resentment, or jealousy. Those feelings only alter your mindset and your spirit, but they will not alter the person to whom you direct them.

If you choose to operate in the mindset that someone else does not deserve what they received or what they have, you are relying on a false belief system. You incorrectly believe your happiness is determined by getting what others have for yourself.

Only when you celebrate in other people's triumphs will you develop a deep inner joy and peace that will spring up and bestow the value of integrity in your life.

If you are in a leadership position, or seeking a leadership position, you must recognize that there may be occasions when you might experience jealousy, disappointment, ambition, insecurities, and other human emotions that nearly all of us experience at one time or another.

However, if these emotions are left unchecked, you risk impacting your team negatively and reducing the overall morale.

When you see jealousy or envy from one of your team members, take these steps:

1. **Address the situation immediately in order to put a stop to the behavior.**
    Don't gloss over the problem. Address it directly to find out the cause of the envy or jealousy.

2. **Remove the person from your department if necessary, so they don't sink your ship.**

   The person may feel threatened that someone will take over their position or fill a potential promotion that they feel belongs to them. Or, they may be angry that someone else is outperforming them. You can assist by identifying the exact cause of the underlying problem. For instance, if the person feels that someone is outperforming them, you can help them by:

   - Identifying how the other person is over-performing.
   - Encouraging them to work with the person who is over-performing to learn from them on how to be more effective. The under-performing worker(s) can implement these practices within their own work, so they, too, can experience greater success.

And if it doesn't work, you may have to reconfigure your department or start the firing process for the person who can't get over their jealousy.

Treat Your Employees Fairly

If you have a concern about someone, don't talk about that concern with someone else. Directly address the person with whom you have a specific problem. For instance, someone I know once fired an employee for engaging in what they considered "immoral behavior"—all based on the say-so of another employee. This ended in a lawsuit. You can't fire an employee for what they do on their free time and you can't fire an employee based on a rumor. If this person had spoken directly to the employee in question instead of firing him, he might have saved thousands of dollars in legal fees—and his reputation as a fair employer.

#2

WHEN FLIGHT MAY BE WISER THAN FIGHT

I hope your own circumstances have not been as chilling as my story, but you will face situations in life in which walking away from even a good job will be the best option for you. The decision to break free poses challenges. Walking away (or running) from a situation may be difficult for many reasons, including these:

1. **They're called "comfort zones" for a reason.**
   Leaving is full of unknowns. How will you handle your financial situation? How will your life change? You may be thinking, "I may not be able to handle the disruption and unknowns if I leave." Or, you may be walking away from a business situation in which you may be comfortable with your colleagues and your income, but the company has asked you to perform an unethical transaction. Sometimes, it may seem easier to remain quiet and stay.

After all, you have a family to support. You cannot afford to lose your job. And what if you don't find another position that pays so well? You may face difficulty emotionally and intellectually in not wanting to get out of your comfort zone and walk away.

2. **Others may think poorly of you.**

You might feel worried that others may think you are a failure at relationships or in business or that they may unjustly and harshly judge you. Keep reading, and you will learn how to trust your voice and rely on your inner strengths, ignoring those who try to inject their venomous thoughts about you into your life. **You are not living their life. You are living your life.** We can't control what others think or believe or how they feel about us, just as they can't control our thoughts. Because this is so, we should care less about what others think. It's their business. And it's your business to make sure you are operating out of your strengths and living a life in which you are able to be a contributor and live a life of abundance.

In fact, what others think about you is none of your business. Yes, I said that, and I meant what I said. Is it anybody's business what you are thinking? No, it is not. Stop worrying about what others think. You cannot change someone else's thought process. That is their concern. Your focus should be on you, not them, not their thoughts about you, not how they think you will fail. Because they do not define your value.

3. **It may lead to loneliness or isolation.**

    You may want out of venomous relationships, but the stinging heartache of being alone seems even more painful. So you rationalize. "My boyfriend was stressed out; he didn't mean what he said." "My wife knocked me out with a frying pan, but it was my fault. I shouldn't have made her angry." Or, "My boss is just looking out for the employees and wants to pay us well. It was a small blunder that anyone could have made," when you realize that he fudged the numbers. But in reality, your boss committed accounting fraud.

#3

STRATEGIES FOR WALKING BACK TO YOU

Following are the strategies that helped me when I walked away and showed me how to trade my dead zombie-like heart for a heart full of life, amid tragedy. And I know they will help you, too.

1. **Discover your strengths.**

    I am a woman of faith, and I am reminded of the uniqueness that is yours and yours alone, created by our Creator. According to Psalm 139:13–14, you are fearfully and wonderfully made, knitted inside your mother's womb. Although we are the same in many ways, we are unique in the way we think and the way we process things and solve problems. In that vein, we all also have our own strengths that we often overlook because we tend to focus on our weaknesses. This exercise will help you to find your inner strength.

What do you do well? List three or more things you do very well.

1. _____

2. _____

3. _____

It may take you some time to list three things, but I guarantee that you have more than three things you are good at. I challenge you to take a separate sheet of paper and begin to jot down everything you can think of that you are good at after you have listed the first three things. You don't have to be a wiz at physics or rocket science, or be as smart as Justice Ruth Bader Ginsberg. It could be, "I make an amazing pecan pie." (I have read that Justice Ginsberg could not cook, so if she had no one to cook for her, being able to cook would have been far more important than being a genius in the law if everyone was hungry!)

Or you can list something a bit more challenging, such as, "I'm a great mom, and I am invested in my children's personal growth, their education, and their spiritual as well as their physical well-being." My point is that there is no skill that is too small or unworthy. Everyone has skills that have value and add value to others. Sure, you may not be on the cover of a magazine, but the skills you have are essential to those around you.

We all face criticism from others, sometimes daily. Sometimes, it even comes from those you love most. Other times, you hold on to past criticism and carry it around like a souvenir.

Here is a challenge: When you remember an old criticism, throw out that thought and replace it with a new thought based on those things that you do very well. When you receive destructive criticism, let it go in one ear and out the other. In other words, don't dwell on that criticism. Focus on what you do well.

2. **Pay attention to how often you think of your past experiences.**

As soon as you become aware that you are thinking of a past painful or hurtful memory, think of where you are right now.

Are you safe? (If the answer is no, get to safety immediately by calling 911 or your local shelter.)

Are you healthy?

Are you okay, right now?

(Please note that if your past experiences are causing too much heartache and pain, you should seek specialized counseling with a therapist who has experience and training in the type of trauma you have suffered.)

Another strategy that I have found helpful is to think on what is true, pure, noble, lovely, good, and praiseworthy **right now**. For example, in the mornings, when my heart was so very hurt, and the pain I experienced was beyond anything I could accurately describe, I began to realize I was focused on the past and on circumstances I could not change. Therefore, over time, I changed the trajectory of my thoughts and focused on the now, the present moment, and gave thanks for what I did have, such as my children, my safety, my health, and quite simply, the blessing of being alive.

We all have the freedom to choose the actions we will take for ourselves or toward others. What this means is that your actions may affect other people, whether positively or negatively. If we did not have free will, we would not be who we are—created to create, created to think, created to design, and created for greater fortune. Whether you believe in God or not, science has proven that only humans have the capacity to choose outside of instincts. To create, design, and contribute to society. To think and determine the direction we take in life. To choose between good and evil. You have that freedom.

Your actions carry immense responsibility because they will impact those around you and create your trajectory in life. Your choices today will define who you become tomorrow. Sadly, when people choose evil, it sometimes impacts those who choose good.

I began to thank God for bringing us to safety. I was thankful that the abuse was now over. The children WERE safe now. We had a roof over our heads—even though we were sleeping on the living room floor, we were not out in the cold under a bridge. I gave thanks for the little things we did have. We had each other. The children were both a gift and a blessing. I looked at what I did receive from the hell we had all lived through, and that hell produced four beautiful lives.

3. **Be grateful.**

I encourage you to write down ten different things you are thankful for, every day. I do this every day. It seems so simple, but it is powerful, and within thirty days, if you follow this simple plan, you will experience a transformational positive mental attitude, despite your adversities. Sometimes the most beautiful experiences in life arise out of difficult circumstances. You may not fully understand the struggles you are facing, but you can trust and have faith; you will find meaning and beauty within the tragedy. The beauty I saw from my involvement in horrifically violent marriages was that four beautiful children were produced.

Look at your adversity as going through a "learning vortex"—when you get out, you will be stronger. If you have survived a storm, you are bound to come out tougher on the other end. Adversity has a way of strengthening us, allowing us to unleash the greater part of ourselves, and releasing the life source that is within us already.

4. **Eliminate guilt.**

Guilt is good for helping us acknowledge our mistakes, but **we need to learn to forgive ourselves and move forward**. I was stuck on guilt. It took me some time to finally recognize the damage this was doing to my spirit. The daily guilt of having married an abuser was never going to change what happened. It was never going to erase the damage that was already done. I had to recognize, too, that I had no idea my husband was an abuser, and as soon as I discovered who he was, I walked away. I had to let the guilt go. If you have any guilt, recognize your mistake, acknowledge what you can do not to repeat it again, and then let it go and move on.

Healing came over time. Reflection and an embracing gratitude helped ease my pain. I realized that I still had many things to be thankful for. I did not have to live in despair. I could choose hope.

5. **Lose the expectations.**

Culture, society, and family place many expectations on us. We are seen as failures if we don't have a perfect marriage, if our kids don't go to private schools, and if we don't drive a nice car. We all have our own paths to travel, and cultural or family expectations will hinder us as we use our challenges to find our way. When I think about expectations, I'm drawn to the story of Lucille Ball. She was told by reviewers, managers, fans, and perhaps even family to find a new profession when her career in movies didn't take off. We all know how her story turned out.

#4

WHEN TRAGEDY LEADS TO OPPORTUNITY

My life often feels like a telenovela, one of those Mexican soap operas beloved by my grandmother. Unfortunately, we cannot grab a remote control and change the channel when drama occurs in our own lives. I have wished that I could do that many times when my real-life drama seemed like a tragic series that would never end.

But what I learned about difficult times is that seeing life situations as opportunities for growth can lead to even greater success, as well as some of the benefits listed below.

1. **Strength in Leaving Your Comfort Zone**
   Walking away from familiarity can be scary. You are likely to experience setbacks, as I did. I left my home, my car, and my six-figure salary for the safety of my children. I had to deal with the loss. Many of us have difficulty not being able to experience immediate results. When you deal with a significant loss, it is likely you will not experience results

right away. Things will become more challenging before they get better. Walking away shows that you do have the strength and fortitude to face hard times. Know that each step you take as you walk away from your comfort zone will help you get through the struggle until you eventually see the results you want. What I have learned is that at the death of nightfall, there lives the promise of a brighter, more joyful morning.

2. **A Sense of Your True Identity**

    When you break free from worrying about what others think, you gain strength. Many of us have a deep desire for outside approval. We want to be valued and loved, and we wish for our lives to have meaning. **But we will not find these things outside of ourselves.** We find them within. Within the greater you. Yes—inside the greater you, there is a treasure.

3. **Inner Peace**

    Sure, walking away may leave you a bit lonelier while facing new challenges, but you will gain inner peace knowing that you stood your ground and your strength was unleashed. You were not afraid of losing. And, when you are not scared of failing, you have nothing else to fear, resulting in inner comfort that can only be found in the greater you.

THREE

STAND UP

s noted in the introduction, I am a small woman. For better or worse, I have always looked younger than my age. It is also true that I have a soft speaking voice. Maybe for these reasons, I have often been underestimated. Most of the time, I have been able to use this to my advantage, including times when businesspeople tried to take advantage of me. It surprises them when I stand my ground, demand respect, and basically show them how I expect to be treated.

So, after hearing the demeaning (and sexist) words and considering my dual-minority situation (Hispanic and female), I refused to back down. I pointed my finger in the president's face and said, "Oh, yeah, just watch me! Give me a thirty-day contract, straight commission. If I don't sell anything, you can tear up the contract. You have nothing to lose."

He laughed and said, "You have some nerve for such a small person. I've been in this business for twenty years, and I know what it takes. You don't have it. I doubt I will ever see you again, but I will give you your contract, straight commission. You have thirty days."

At that point, the vice president of the company felt compelled to chime in. "You won't be able to sell to doctors because you will have to take them out to the strip clubs or go fishing or hunting to close these large deals. Are you willing to go out to the strip club?"

"You are right," I replied. "I am not willing to go to the strip club or go fishing and hunting, but I've never had to do that to close a deal, and I won't start now. But I can guarantee you that if I could close a $150,000 government contract and run a $600 million marketing budget, I can definitely sell a $35,000 piece of equipment without having to go to strip clubs."

After throwing down the gauntlet at my training session, I was determined to refuse to allow anyone to classify my value, skills, or talents. I knew me. I knew what I had accomplished.

As soon as I returned home to McAllen, I started making calls, fueled by my desire to prove the executives wrong as well as, more importantly, to provide for my family. Then, my personal life faced another storm.

Upon returning home, I was told that my grandfather was in the hospital fighting for his life. He had always been conscientious about his health. He watched his diet carefully, eating organic foods, and exercised daily. While my grandmother drove to work every day, he walked to work to get as much exercise in the day as he could. He had gone in for his annual checkup feeling fine but had been diagnosed with leukemia. By the time I returned, my grandfather was already undergoing chemotherapy.

I knew I had four weeks to make sales, but I also had no idea how much time my grandpa had left. I had to be there for him. I wouldn't have survived my teen years without him. He had always been the one man in my life I could count on. He always had my back. So, I went to the hospital every day to sit by his bedside as his condition rapidly deteriorated.

I was there when he died nearly three weeks later. Between caring for him and my children, I had no time to make sales calls. I had delusions that the president would be understanding and give me more time, but during the week of my grandfather's funeral, he called.

"Your time is up, little girl. You haven't made any sales. We are canceling your contract," he said.

"I still have one more week," I replied. "My grandpa just passed away, and I have not been able to make sales calls, but I have one week left to meet my quota."

"Yeah, right," he said, as he laughed.

"You agreed to thirty days, and I still have a week on my contract, and I will meet my quota," I said.

"Sure you will," he said sarcastically. Then he snickered and as he hung up the phone.

I knew I needed to be seriously disciplined in my approach to have any chance of meeting my quota.

～

I prayed like a woman on fire as I made one cold call after another to doctors all over the Rio Grande Valley. I made hundreds of calls without getting a single appointment until my last day, Friday.

With the clock ticking to zero, Dr. Benjamin Jones agreed to see me. Maybe I was desperate, but he was a great prospect, and I was going to jump on the opportunity.

Dr. Jones was leaving a large group and starting his own practice. He didn't lack for ambition and was opening six clinics across the valley.

"I will meet my quota after closing this doctor," I thought after confirming the appointment.

I put on my nicest dress for our meeting at his new office. The office was so new that he didn't have any furniture beyond a couple of rolling stools. He sat on one, and I took the other as I made my presentation. I had just launched into my well-practiced spiel when I began to feel the stool slip and roll out from under me.

I tried to stand up but couldn't get my balance as the stool shot out from under me. I went over backward with my legs flying up in the air. I found myself on my back with my dress up almost to my waist and my potential customer standing over me with a very concerned look on his face.

"Are you okay?" Dr. Jones asked as he helped me to my feet.

I would like to think it was my skillful and knowledgeable presentation that secured the deal that day, but I admit Dr. Jones might just have felt sorry for me. Whatever his motivation, he signed up for not one, but six, of our devices at $35,000 each.

I closed the sale and met my quota in that somewhat disastrous meeting.

———

"Marie, he probably gave you a bad check," the company president said, laughing. "That's just too good to be true. The check will have to clear our bank before you can join the sales team."

The check cleared.

I reached my quota for the next three months and set the record for the most units sold in that period.

Now, I have to admit that there was no way I could have expected to find one doctor who would buy so many medical devices, especially after I fell on my you-know-what during my sales pitch. But that's the point! You never know what can happen, good or bad. **But as long as you keep trying, there will be opportunities to succeed.** And I've found that one opportunity often leads to another and another and another. Goes to show that falling (even hard on your butt) can lead to greater blessings.

On my one-year anniversary, I was named the company's national sales rep of the year.

CHAPTER THREE
LESSONS AND GUIDES

#1

THINGS TO REMEMBER WHEN STANDING UP FOR YOURSELF

1. **Remember Your Value**

   Head back to your list of strengths from page 47. Referring back to this will help you build your confidence. Constantly thinking about and reassessing your skills, talents, and contributions will enable you to understand your value. And when you need to stand up for yourself, speak from your strengths. There's no need to embellish. Remember, there will never be another you.

2. **Don't Confuse Confidence with Arrogance**

   Throughout this book, I share a lot about my accomplishments. And I do so confidently. Please know that **I am sharing to impress *upon you*, not impress you**. There's a difference. Arrogant people believe that they are smarter, better, more attractive, or more valuable than others. No one likes arrogance. Meanwhile, confidence is your ability to acknowledge you have value—but not more than those around you . . . and certainly not less. Confidence has nothing to do with your level of skill, education, or the size of your bank account. Arrogant people place value on individuals based on a materialistic point of view and based on one's level of education, instead of on the intrinsic value we all possess.

3. **Stand Your Ground**

   Regardless of your position or title, you can always develop the ability to defeat challenges that seem bigger than you. Like the story of David and Goliath, lack of "size" is not a limitation, unless you allow **others** to set limits on you. Choose to be a David among the Goliaths you face in life.

4. **Refuse to Be Identified as Anything Other Than Your True Self**

   Only you know you. You know your heart. You know your strengths. You know your value. Never allow anyone else take that knowledge and self-assurance away from you. When you allow someone else to define your identity for you, you lose self-respect, confidence, and your sense of self-worth—especially when that negative judgment comes from someone in authority. Only give yourself the permission to define you. People in positions of power (or anyone, for that matter) do not create identities unless you allow them to. I trust that you will walk, talk, and act within your own identity! So, teach yourself to stop worrying about what others think. **You cannot force change on someone else's thought process. That is their concern. Your focus should be on you, not them.** No matter your faith system, you have to admit that we all have complex language and thinking processes that allow us to communicate with other humans to build collaborative relationships. That means you have the ability to act outside of instinct and to create, think, design, and determine the course of your own life. Someone else's estimation of you cannot take that away . . . unless you let it.

5. **Break Through Walls**

Depending on which news station you are listening to, you are either in support of building walls for protection or tearing down walls for freedom. I am not referring to those types of walls. I am speaking to the walls you and I face every day: the unseen barriers hindering our personal or professional progress. These types of walls are always meant to be scaled. And as a tiny Hispanic woman, I felt like I had to crush these professional barriers before they crushed me. At times, the ladder you create to climb these walls will collapse and you may end up flat on your back. Put up a new, improved ladder. Do whatever it takes. Make it your mission . . . for yourself and those who will follow in your footsteps.

This may be the most difficult barrier to stand up to. You will need to face derogatory comments such as: "Who do you think you are?" "You don't have the talent." "You don't have the looks." "You don't have the money." "Just give up." "You'll never make it." "You are so stupid." "Your voice sounds funny."

And even worse than that is when you forget about the aforementioned lessons in step 4, and you end up building the wall by yourself—each brick a negative comment that you have internalized.

#2

LAUGH AT YOURSELF

Learn to smile. Learn to laugh. When you laugh, you reveal to the world what is inside of you. It certainly helped when I fell off that stool.

One of the medical devices I obtained FDA clearance for was able to measure mental and physical stress, along with more than seventy-five various conditions. Mental stress is measured by your ability to handle stress, which is further measured via various biological markers.[1] Whether you are experiencing positive or negative emotions, your body produces chemicals that impact its ability to return to a normal state. With negative emotions such as being bitter, sad, vengeful, worried, or upset, your body produces adverse chemicals that impact your body in such a way that the chemicals produce chaos and result in difficulty maintaining balance of your autonomic nervous system and maintaining homeostasis.

In addition, the imbalance creates chaos within your body that if prolonged could begin to impact you on a physical level as well. Studies indicate that chronic stress carried over on a daily

basis may result in damage to the immune system. Other consequences of carried-over stress include depression, anxiety, ulcers,
sleep disorders, cancers, stomach and heart disorders, plus much
more. None of us are immune to stress, and in fact, all of us go
through life with some form of stress on a daily basis. From being
stressed out with our workload, occasional illness, relationship
problems, or other concerns, the key to survival is how we handle
the stress. If you are unable to let go of harm done to you and
remain angry and unforgiving toward the one who has harmed
you for up to six months, that may result in cumulative stress,
which will begin to impact you physically as well as mentally. Or,
perhaps you can't let go of a mistake you made in the past and you
carry guilt in your heart. This is also very harmful to your system.[3]

Being able to smile and laugh at life's storms and difficulties
creates a sense of calm in your body, resulting in the production
of chemicals that enable your body to return to homeostasis. Just
as the palm tree grows stronger after the storm, laughter in the
face of adversity can make you stronger than you were before.

If you do not learn to laugh at yourself, or your circumstances,
others will help you do it. A competitor once hacked into our
website and turned it into an Asian dating site. My daughter and
everyone else I told just laughed and laughed. I couldn't understand what was so funny about that! We had a serious company,
a medical product that required we maintain the highest level of
government compliance with the FDA, and they were laughing
that clinicians were finding an Asian dating website instead of
our diagnostic devices that helped patients! Eventually, I found
the humor in the situation and was then able to focus on getting

our website back to where it needed to be and implement stricter defenses against breaches and hacks.

On another occasion, I was speaking for the American Marketing Association in Cincinnati. It was a cool day in March 2019, so I was wearing boots. I had also driven up from Dayton, a short one-hour drive. But I was super thirsty and didn't have time to stop by the store to grab a drink. I figured they would have refreshments during the event. All they had was coffee, which is expected, because it was early in the morning. However, I don't drink coffee. Water was not offered, and as I was going up to speak, I desperately needed to drink something for my dry mouth, so I gulped down some coffee, which made me jittery.

To make matters worse, I suddenly felt one leg was shorter! My boot heel fell off during my presentation! So, here I was in front of the audience hopping around with one shorter leg because of my broken heel and jittery hands due to the coffee that I had gulped down. Again, we all laughed and joked about it; at least I was able to give them free entertainment.

I rarely wear fake eyelashes. However, I had an interview with NEXtv, a popular Spanish station in Panamá, and my friend convinced me to wear fake eyelashes so that I could look my best in front of the cameras. Unfortunately, during the interview, I felt one of the fake eyelashes loosen. Half of it was off and I could feel it flapping; it was so uncomfortable. I was not sure if I should remove it, as we were on live TV, or to not mess with it, hoping no one would see it, yet I was constantly blinking my eyes! To make matters worse, I had not planned for the interview, which was in Spanish, and my Spanish is limited! Although I am Hispanic, Spanish is my second language. English was the primary language spoken at home while I was growing up—and the only Spanish I was exposed to was Spanglish!

Fortunately, I survived the interview and the host was so gracious. He noticed my eyelash, but assured me that the audience was not able to see it. We got a good laugh and he enjoyed the interview so much, he insisted I conduct more interviews with additional TV and radio stations. I felt like going back to my room and hiding the rest of the trip, but that would not serve anyone, and I was there to serve, so I just laughed it off and we were able to move on.

I've had so many embarrassing moments, some worse than those mentioned here, but I've learned to use these moments as an opportunity to laugh. There may be times when you have embarrassing moments, possibly worse than mine, but laughing at them will help you to persevere. Crying, feeling bad for yourself, or blaming yourself for things outside of your control does not serve you or others, and will only distract you from your purpose.

#3

MY PRINCIPLES FOR SUCCESS

I used the following principles to help take me from almost being let go before I even got started to climbing to number one in sales nationally. I still use these to help me achieve any goal I set for myself.

1. Get Disciplined

Are you disciplined enough to do what it takes during your downtime to help you reach success?

I had only one week left to meet my quota. I had four small children to support. I had no other option than to be disciplined with my time. Although being a single parent rarely provides extra downtime, the downtime I did have after getting the kids to bed early was spent on carefully planning the next day. I decided on which doctors to call and determined the best time to call. I studied all the available information on sales. I awakened extra early to prepare before dropping off the kids to school, and then started making sales calls. What you do with your downtime helps determine your level of success.

Legendary Dallas Cowboys football coach Tom Landry once said, "The job of a football coach is to make men do what they don't want to do in order to achieve what they always wanted to be." Successful people are disciplined people, and for most, success did not occur overnight.

Unfortunately, we live in a society that uses a "microwave mentality," maintaining that if you do not see instant results, you are a failure. When my twenty-seven-year-old was a teenager, he practiced his guitar and piano each morning before and after school. He taught himself to play, and then started writing his own music and later producing music for others. He formed a band.

One day, he told me that he had to get rid of one of his band members. When I asked why, he said that, ever since the band had started playing shows, this member saw no need to continue practicing; he had "made it to the stage." However, lack of practice caused him to mess up during live performances. He lacked the discipline to maintain and enhance his skills.

My son remains passionate about his music. He realizes that he cannot become the best version of himself without the discipline required to put in the necessary practice time.

2. **Be Determined**

Vince Lombardi, another legendary football coach, said, "The price of success is hard work, dedication to the job at hand, and the determination that whether we win or lose, we have applied the best of ourselves to the task at hand."

I was determined to prove that I could meet my quota in one week. It was a long shot, I knew. But if I put in the effort and dedication, and remained determined, I knew that I was putting in the very best of myself to reach my goal.

Writing down and contemplating the following will help you grow in your determination to reach your goal:

What goal, vision, dream, or desire do you really want? What it is that you really want must carry with it an intense desire, emotionally and intellectually.

Who inspires you? Sylvester Stallone was someone who inspired me to look at a situation with the belief that, regardless of how grim the odds seem, the American Dream is possible. During a 1976 interview, he recalled watching a Muhammad Ali fight. "I was watching the fight in a movie theater," he said, "and I said to myself, 'Let's talk about stifled ambition and broken dreams and people who sit on the curb looking at their dreams go down the drain.' I thought about it for a month. That's what I call my inspiration stage. Then I let it incubate for ten months, the incubation stage. Then came the verification stage, when I wrote it in 3½ days. I'd get up at 6 a.m. and write it by hand, with a Bic pen on lined notebook sheets of paper. Then my wife, Sasha, would type it. She kept saying, 'You've gotta do it, you've gotta do it. Push it, Sly, go for broke.'"[4]

For Sylvester Stallone, it was watching a fight that inspired him to write the *Rocky* movie screenplay in three-and-half days, which ultimately took him from "Roaches to Riches." He went from having a starving dog, living in a roach-infested apartment, to becoming a huge American success story. You, too, can glean inspiration from something you see, someone you know, or someone you know of, who has overcome tragedy and experienced triumph.

3. **Take Action**

Too often, we simply dream of what is possible. We dream of a better tomorrow. But if we do not take action toward our dreams, they will merely remain dreams. Taking action will help you build that determination muscle you need to reach your goals. Have your big goal in mind. But also create smaller goals to achieve your larger goal. Then create actionable steps to reach your small goals, and eventually you will reach your larger goal.

For example, my goal was to earn $1 million a year. I broke that goal down into monthly chunks, then weekly, then daily, and then hourly. I calculated how many sales I would need to make in one year to earn one million dollars. I knew I could not do this all at once; therefore, I divided the goal into monthly sales, weekly sales, and daily sales. When I looked at the number of sales I needed to make in one year to earn a million dollars, it seemed like an impossible task. However, when I broke it down to see how many sales I needed to make in a week, it seemed doable. Then, I took action to make the sales calls and close deals to reach my goals.

4. **Don't Give Up**

Work with determination to complete your goal. It may seem that you keep facing challenge after challenge. It may seem impossible. But too often we give up too early. I could have just accepted my fate when I was told that my time was up and they were canceling my contract. After all, one week is hardly enough time, especially for someone like me who did not have the years of experience other sales representatives had in the medical field. But what I did have was the dedication not to give up: to keep going, to pursue my goal until the very end!

5. Be Dedicated

My dedication to supporting my children, providing for their medical care, and lifting us off my aunt and uncle's living room floor gave me the push I needed to succeed.

You may be thinking, "I don't have time to set my goals; I simply have too much going on!" My grandmother, who fought so hard for my mom's life and mine, passed away recently at the age of ninety-five. I learned of her death right before I was scheduled to go onstage in Atlanta. I had also planned to stay an extra day for business. However, I immediately cancelled all my plans to attend my grandmother's funeral service. Isn't it interesting that when there is a family emergency, we find the time to take care of what needs to be taken care of? Somehow you find a way no matter what it takes. In my case, there were no flights to get me to Texas from Atlanta, nor were there flights to get me there in the morning before the funeral service. I ended up driving. There was no way I was going to miss paying my final respects to my grandmother, who was responsible for me being here.

I am also reminded of a few sales representatives who are on a hybrid pay scale of commissions plus salary. They will sometimes get lazy and not sell anything until they get behind on their payments. At that time, they call me and ask me to help them "close" a sale, because it is a self-created emergency and they need to make their car or house payment. They end up closing a lot of deals and earning enough to keep them going for the next six months. But, as soon as the pressure is off, they stop working hard. They lose that discipline, determination, and dedication to maintain the lifestyle they want to keep— and the cycle repeats itself.

One sales rep was taken off salary and put on straight commission. He had the ability to make sales, but he would make just enough effort to make a few sales calls a week and not put in the hours he was getting paid. For instance, he would work only twenty to twenty-five hours, but he was getting a full-time, forty-hour salary. We had no choice but to take him off salary, since he felt entitled to determine his own hours. Since he began working on straight commission, we see more sales coming from him than before.

With discipline, determination, and dedication, you will surely be a winner. It was not easy being disciplined to do the hard work and committing myself to take action, but it was necessary because the dedication required to support my children was overpowering. I was going to make sure that nothing hindered me from giving them a better life and preventing the horror they had experienced from ever happening to them again.

To whom or what are you dedicated? Always keep that answer close to your heart so you will remain focused on the reason why you need to achieve your goal, dream, or vision for your future.

6. Seize Opportunities as They Present Themselves

Learning to seize the opportunity, regardless of the situation, will lead to success.

During a workshop where I spoke, one of my fellow speakers pulled out a bunch of bills from his pocket and said, "I have some free money for whoever wants to come up and grab it."

Very few people came up. He asked the audience, "Why did you not come up?"

The answers were varied.

"I was too far away. By the time I got there, the money would have been all gone."

"I didn't know the denomination. If they were dollar bills, it was not worth going up."

"I didn't know if it was real money."

"I was afraid of tripping on my way up there."

"I was embarrassed to get up in front of a bunch of strangers."

When the audience realized that it was real money, and they were NOT one-dollar bills, they regretted their inaction. The speaker pulled out more money. He said, "I'm giving away more money—come up and get it."

Almost the entire room ran up to grab what they could.

That's what it's like in real life. We are afraid to take risks. We are afraid to seize an opportunity because of the unknown.

#4

DEADEN THE VOICES

Difficulties will always be there, but if you refuse to give up, opportunities to succeed will emerge. You never know what can happen, good or bad, but as long as you keep trying, those opportunities will be within your grasp. And I've found that one opportunity often leads to another, then another and another. A chance at creating your own success story is everywhere; you just need to look for it and seize it. The following steps can help you develop the skills needed to learn how to seize opportunity toward success:

1. **Look at the Possibilities, Not the Impossibilities**

    I have found that impossibilities are opportunities for greater possibilities. For example, when I realized I only had one week left to make a sale, the president of the company was just looking at the difficulty of the task and didn't think I could make it. I looked at the possibility. I had one week of possibility. It was an opportunity I was willing to take. Many people would have agreed with the CEO and would have forfeited their moment.

2. **Accept That You Don't Have to Know It All**

    Not knowing it all may be risky, and you may fail. Zig Ziglar said, "You don't have to be great to start, but you have to start to be great." Get started; take action, even if you don't know it all. I certainly didn't know everything there was to know about sales, the product I was selling, or all the medical phraseology. That required years of learning, growing, and investing in myself. I am still learning today. But I took action and started selling right away, knowing I would fail, again and again, until I finally got a "Yes" on that very last day. Today, I continue to face challenges. I still don't know it all. But what I do know is that as long as I keep trying, taking action, and maintaining a teachable spirit, I will find possibility even in the not knowing.

3. **Deaden the Voices That Break Your Spirit**

You will have to stifle all the negative voices from your past and move on. Ever since I was a child, I've been told that my voice wasn't good enough. Today, I travel internationally, speaking to large audiences with Nick Vujicic, Les Brown, John Maxwell, and many other well-known motivational speakers. I have yet to be told to put a muzzle on it. In fact, when I was in Panamá speaking at "La Ciudad de Saber" (The City of Knowledge), I was initially going to speak for one day; then I was asked to stay a second day. After my second talk, I was asked to speak for three more days. Dignitaries from the US embassy, educators, and entrepreneurs came to every talk I gave. I share this with you not to build myself up but to impress upon you that, yes, it is possible for you regardless of what perceived limitations you believe you have.

In kindergarten, I was told by one of my aunts, "Don't sing. You have a terrible voice. Make sure you only lip-sync when you are in music class. You don't ever want any-one, especially the teacher, to hear you sing." I lip-synced through music class every year after that, and I regret it because now I know that singing is something you can learn to do, and I missed out by never practicing. As a side note, it has been said that only one person in ten thousand has perfect pitch. Yet, a music instructor in Japan, Kazuko Eguchi, began working with kids younger than four years old to teach them perfect pitch. He has taught more than eight hundred teachers his method, and today they have a nearly 100 percent success rate in teaching perfect pitch to children! Perfect pitch stays with them for life.[5]

Many of the "limitations" we believe we have may have come from our past: from people with a lack of awareness who may have implanted the idea that we have such limitations—and we then took that misguided idea as "truth."

JUMP!

After around three years of successfully selling medical devices for the company that thought I would never make it, I received a fax that would change my life. We'd lost the contract to sell the device!

Even worse, I then received another fax from my company warning that anyone who signed up to sell directly for the manufacturer would be sued. Wow! I had worked so hard to become number one in sales. I was at a loss. I contacted my lawyer to review the opportunities and the obstacles. On one hand, the manufacturer was indeed offering me a contract doubling the amount of commissions I had been making with the distributor. On the other hand, the distribution company's contract I'd signed prohibited me from working with the manufacturer directly. The language was clear. I pleaded with the attorney, "If I can't sell for the distributor, because they lost their contract, doesn't that give me the right to sell for the manufacturer?" He said, "No, it's a solid contract. The only choice you have is to find another job or sell a completely different product or in another industry."

I believed these restrictions were grossly unfair. How could I be prohibited from earning a living? Some of the other sales reps decided to sell directly for the manufacturer. They ended up in lengthy lawsuits. I was a single mother of four. I could not afford to be sued.

I quickly learned that while you can do very well financially in medical capital equipment sales via commissions, the entire field is like the Wild, Wild West. There is no government regulation and no certification process for medical device sales representatives. Furthermore, while medical devices are subject to heavy regulatory compliance, the machines themselves are never tested directly by the FDA. There is virtually no code of ethics. "Cutthroat" doesn't begin to describe the level of competition or the working environment. Job security is nonexistent and biases run rampant in this industry.

Though I considered myself relatively savvy, given my experiences up to that point, I still was very much a babe in the woods in this world. Not only that, but my success, despite my inexperience, made me a target, not only for my competitors but also from within my own company.

For instance, my commissions varied, depending on the device and its makers. Some paid $4,000 in commission. Others paid $15,000 to $18,000. The companies we represented were sometimes in direct competition with each other, creating a contentious environment.

The field also included unethical companies that would get shut down for fraud or deception or some other serious violation, only to soon be back in business under a different name a few weeks later. I know of one manufacturer that has operated under at least five different names.

⸺

My lessons in the Wild West of medical devices sales didn't end there. Unable to sell the device that had gotten my family and me back on solid ground, I began to do research on other products in the medical field that did not break my contract.

I found a very interesting company that focused on dizziness disorders. As an independent distributor, I began to sell many of their devices. Then, one day, they sent me a commission for less than half of what I should have received. Worse, they sent me the check two weeks late. I had mounting medical bills for my kids. I remember during that time period that it seemed as though everything was going wrong for me. On top of my kids' medical bills, I ended up with pneumonia. I could not afford the doctor's visit, but fortunately, with the relationships I had built within the industry, a physician agreed to see me for free. The only problem was that I could not afford my medication. I called the company I was selling for and pleaded with them in a whisper, because I had already lost my voice, "Please, can you just send me my check? I need the funds immediately to pay for my medication." The owners flat out said, "NO!"

When I did finally receive my check, I asked them why my commission was so low. They replied, "Our costs went up, so we had to take it out of your commission."

I could not continue working for a company that so blatantly and unethically changed the rules and broke contracts to suit their needs. I searched for other companies to sell for and discovered a medical device manufacturing company called balanceback.

—

I liked balanceback because they were in the process of going to market with a product that helped to diagnose and treat vestibular, balance, and central nervous system (CNS) disorders, including brain injuries, concussions, and migraines. My mother had suffered a serious brain injury, and I loved the idea of getting involved with a company that helped people like her.

I placed a phone call and was able to secure an interview. I traveled to meet with the developers of the products who were some of the top scientists and clinicians in the world. I was impressed. Fortunately, I had enough experience to be able to get a contract to sell their products throughout the US. However, it was not that easy to secure a contract. First, balanceback felt that the previous company I had worked for was not ethical. I was told, "We don't work with people who come from the 'dark side.'" I agreed. I didn't think it was ethical to cut someone's pay without telling them! I explained what happened to me, and that I did not realize they were not a very ethical company prior to my personal experiences. They agreed to give me a chance to prove myself.

I was so excited with my new job selling balanceback devices. I was fascinated by the fact that their hardware and software had been developed by an engineer who had once served as a division manager at the Air Force Research Laboratory. He had developed in-flight systems for high-performance fighter aircraft, including managing the development of state-of-the-art flight control systems for the F16, X29, Predator, and F15. He'd also collaborated with the top clinicians in the world to engineer the world's best diagnostic system for balance disorders. This company had relationships with the top universities, military bases, and hospitals in the country, some of which had conducted clinically validated research on the product.

As soon as balanceback's product launched, I made their very first sale. I soon became the company's top sales rep. The income was great! I was selling four to six devices a month and giving doctors an alternative to prescribing pharmacological treatment for dizziness that had a high failure rate. Financial and business success gave me the confidence to persevere through other challenges that came. I felt like I could bounce back from almost anything.

Prior to this patented invention, clinicians could only guess at the cause of dizziness. Patients could go up to five years without correct diagnosis. Yet, the genius clinicians and engineers developed a system that could accurately provide an objective diagnosis in a short office visit so that they could then provide treatment with a 99 percent cure rate.

I was passionate about being part of a collaborative team concerned enough about patient care to make clinicians' jobs easier, more effective, and more rewarding. My passion helped them in their practice of successfully providing outcome-based patient care.

⌒

After two years, one of the members of the partnership that owned balanceback called me. Though we later became good friends, he seemed very condescending and arrogant at that point.

"We really don't think someone without a college degree should be selling directly to doctors. They need to be dealing with someone educated like them," he said.

"What do you mean?" I replied. "I'm your top sales rep. Not having a degree has never stopped me from gaining the respect of my clients and building relationships, resulting in sales!"

He replied, "We don't need you; we could make all of the sales ourselves. They only buy because we have a great product."

I was so offended after that call that I immediately contacted another owner of balanceback, Oscar Espinal, and told him what had just been conveyed to me. His response was, "Marie, don't worry about it. You are doing a great job. This guy says crazy stuff. Just ignore him."

A few months passed, and I still had my job. In fact, I had just closed a big sale for the neurology department at Baylor

University, and another at the University of Texas at Austin. Just after that sale, I received another call from balanceback . . . a different partner this time, who served as the company's vice president.

"Marie, we are so proud of the work you are doing. I'd like to take you out to lunch. I'll be flying into Texas so we can meet while you are doing the installation and training for the neurologist at Baylor."

I completed the equipment installation and training at Baylor, with the same post-sale work remaining at the University of Texas. The only thing on my mind was, "Promotion. Promotion. Promotion." I was positive I would be offered a higher position in the company, maybe even stock options. It was obvious this partner appreciated my work and did not agree with the statements of the partner who thought I needed a college degree to sell their products. Or so I thought.

We met at one of my favorite steak houses. The meeting was going so well, with me being the recipient of many praises of the great job I was doing. I was showing the partner how I used my site-seller. This was a document/program that I created from scratch that showed how I made sales presentations and how I closed sales. It also detailed how I overcame just about any objection that came my way, and how it helped me close sales. The partner liked the work I was doing so much that he asked if I could provide the company with this program. He even offered to pay for it. I wasn't so eager to share this information with the company, so I asked for more time to consider how much I would charge. Creating the program had taken many hours, and I'd developed it over time based on my experiences making presentations and closing sales.

Then he made another offer.

"Marie, you are doing so well, we'd like to put you on salary."

He wrote the offer down and told me to think about it. To my astonishment, I was being offered just about the same amount of money I already earned per month as a yearly salary! This was one of those times that I had to stand my ground. I'd already proven that I was a million-dollar producer in sales, so there was no way I was settling for less.

I said, "I have four kids to support as a single mother. I simply can't afford to accept your salary offer. I will stay on commission."

What the owners of the company didn't understand was that I had no financial support to fall back on. I also had a tremendous amount of medical expenses. My oldest son required physical therapy three times a week. He also required monthly blood work for the autoimmune condition he suffered from. All of us were in counseling due to the horrific abuse that had been inflicted on my children. I, too, was suffering from unrelenting guilt for them having gone through what they did. I needed counseling to help me realize that it was not anything I could control and had to be able to let go of that guilt. Additionally, I needed to travel with all my children and a nanny when we did out-of-town trips. For several years, I homeschooled, as that was the only way I was able to handle my business travel—and take my children with me. Plus, I paid for all my own marketing.

Eleanor Roosevelt once said, "A woman is a like a tea bag. You can't tell how strong she is until you put her in hot water." Well, I was about to get into some very hot water, because after I said that I could not accept the offer, I was told, "If you don't accept the salary, then you can't sell for us anymore."

He basically told me that I was fired. I was also told, "Don't bother going to the University of Texas to do the training; we'll handle it."

I decided that this was a time to jump into what I really wanted in my life.

CHAPTER FOUR
LESSONS AND GUIDES

#1

DON'T BE DISCOURAGED IF YOU DON'T SEE IMMEDIATE RESULTS

Do not be discouraged if you do not see immediate results. Progress may be slow at first, but if you persist in your goals, the result of your efforts will be clearly visible. Sometimes results take time. For example, if a parent were to leave their son a Rolls-Royce as an inheritance, it may be many years before the son is able to drive it. Why? Because maybe the son is only eight years old at the time the parent gave the gift and has no idea what to do with it. It may take years for the son to grow in stature, maturity, wisdom, and experience before he is able to drive it. In the same way, sometimes you may not be ready to reach the goal you desire. You, too, may need time to grow in wisdom and experience. For example, some people give up on their goal of becoming a supervisor at their place of employment too soon. They become discouraged about being overlooked for a promotion, quit, and get a job somewhere else. The cycle continues, and the person feels that life is not fair. The reality is that the person may not have given their employer an opportunity to see their skills, or perhaps the employee hasn't stayed long enough to gain the experience or wisdom necessary to fill the role that they seek.

#2

NEVER TOO OLD, NEVER TOO YOUNG

While speaking to a group of retired executives in Dayton, Ohio, not so long ago, a retired pastor told me that the only reason he retired was because his church told him he was too old to continue serving. But he didn't feel old, and that was why he was at the conference I was facilitating. He wanted to keep growing and didn't want to stay at home doing nothing.

Henry Ford said, "Anyone who stops learning is old, whether at twenty or eighty. Anyone who keeps learning stays young. The greatest thing in life is to keep your mind young."

I agree with Henry Ford. In fact, science now proves that what Ford said is definitely true. In fact, one of the devices balanceback manufactures is a combination of a software program and hardware that forces you to use your core, legs, arms, and entire body, along with your auditory and visual perception combined with cognitive function. Through a series of baseline tests and therapy sessions, you are able to create new neuropathways in the brain. Why? Because you are using your brain and providing the therapy needed to learn and create new connections to make you cognitively smarter and brighter while improving your brain health.

When my now adult son was in high school, he fell from the second story of a building. Prior to his fall, he wanted to join a music class to learn to play piano. He was told he was not good enough and to stick to choir if he wanted anything to do with music. After his accident, he was hospitalized for two weeks with a serious concussion. The neurologist said his brain will never be the same again, and he would suffer serious cognitive deficiencies. This meant that it was possible he would never play music again. Today, he writes, composes, and produces his own classical compositions. They are so beautiful, and they have been performed by orchestras around the country to audiences as large as nine thousand. And today, he performs for social and leadership events (www.justinryanruiz.com). He was able to accomplish this by exercising his brain and rebuilding new pathways in the brain . . . a process many physicians once thought to be impossible.

So, whether you are twenty or one hundred, you have access to the fountain of youth. What is that fountain of youth? It's learning! It keeps your brain function young, youthful, and full of life! With a sharp brain, you can discover fulfillment at any age!

In fact, the concept of retirement is a relatively new concept that started with Otto von Bismarck in Germany, who decided to introduce retirement for citizens reaching seventy years of age.[1] The US decided to follow suit years later when President Franklin D. Roosevelt proposed the Social Security Act of 1935. It took years before Americans accepted the idea of retirement.

A recent study by the Institute of Labor Economics found that "decreased mental activity results in atrophy of cognitive skills."[2] In addition, "retirement plays a significant role in explaining cognitive decline at an older age." The reason this occurs is because in retirement you use less of your cognition, and generally many retirees become isolated, resulting in a significant decline in social interactions.[3] Social interactions play a big part in keeping our brains active, as do reading, writing, and participating in life.

A Canadian physician, Dr. William Osler, was convinced that we produced our best work before the age of forty, and that by sixty we should retire. He said that people over sixty were "useless and should be put out to pasture."[4] As you can probably surmise, I strongly disagree with Osler.

However, our culture has an infatuation with youthfulness. In fact, we are now seeing "motivational" speakers in their teens, who have ample enthusiasm, but no real-world experience. I have met young people who act closer to the end of life than a ninety-year-old woman I know who is more fit than the average teenager. She exercises every day, mentally and physically.

Now, I don't value one particular age over another; to me, it's all about your character and what you are doing to contribute to society. You can do this at any age. My point is this—please don't make age an excuse. You are never too young or too old to unleash greater fortune in your life.

Here are some examples of success that had nothing to do with age:

- Colonel Sanders started franchising KFC at age sixty-two after lots of hard work on his famous recipe! I sure do love my Kentucky Fried Chicken and can't imagine growing up without it!

- One of America's most famous painters, Grandma Moses, started painting later in life and got her big break in her seventies. She was self-taught and painted over a thousand pieces. Her work became so famous, New York governor Nelson Rockefeller declared September 7, 1960, as Grandma Moses Day.

- Noah Webster was forty-eight when he completed the first version of the dictionary. It took him another twenty-two years to complete the *American Dictionary of the English Language*. He was seventy years old.

- The first version of Roget's Thesaurus was started by Peter Roget when he was sixty-one and finalized when he was seventy-three.

- Oscar Swahn competed in three Olympic games and won six medals. At the 1920 Summer Olympics, he became the oldest athlete to compete in the Olympics at the age of seventy-two. He won a silver medal.

- At the age of twelve, Louis Braille began work on his invention that enabled blind people like him to read, and today it is known as Braille.

- The trampoline was invented by George Nissen at the age of sixteen! I'm truly grateful for Nissen, because I used to absolutely love jumping on the trampoline with my kids!

This represents just a small list of the many people, young and old, who have invented or accomplished great feats! Regardless of your age or circumstances, you still have worthwhile ideas to share with the world. If you still have a heartbeat, you have something to contribute. It's always your time to let your greater fortune shine through.

#3
WHEN THE CHIPS ARE DOWN

You can't always expect the world to be fair, but if you jump toward what you want, you will overcome! Take charge to map your desired path. You have to jump to go after what you want or jump out of what you don't want in life. The following pieces of advice helped me jump into opportunity. I think they will help you, too!

1. **Decide Whether You Will React or Respond**

   Reacting strips you of choices and the ability to jump into what you want in life. It leads you into mindlessness. For example, imagine you are sitting around a fire pit roasting marshmallows. You drop a marshmallow into the fire, and instantly put your hand in to retrieve it. That's reacting. Now, of course, I know you wouldn't put your hand in a fire, but sometimes, **when we quickly and thoughtlessly react to something bad in our lives, we get burned**. But there is a different reaction you can choose. You can jump into faith by responding. Responding is seeing the fire and choosing not to put your hand in it. It is the decision to forgive when you are injured. The decision to have a smile when you feel like frowning. It's the decision to laugh when you want to cry. Responding is thoughtful and reflective. It takes effort to stop that instantaneous reaction to allow a more thoughtful response.

The best way to jump out of what you don't want is to respond. You may have pain, as I did. Plenty of it. But I'm a believer that pain produces power. I could have lashed out in many different ways. I could have remained bitter. I'm sure I could have sued. But I did not have time for a lawsuit—I had four kids to raise. I had no time for bitterness. I had to find a way to earn a living—and quick—in order to support my family. I took that pain of getting fired and (as you'll see in the next chapter) turned it into power. I turned my energy into ideas that would give me the power I needed to support my family.

2. Face the Fear

Sometimes we are afraid to jump into something new, especially after having lost something, be it a relationship, a loved one, a job you loved . . . or perhaps you've had to move to a new city that you are not familiar with. One of the top reasons why we are afraid to jump into something new is because **we are afraid of failing**. We are afraid that, if we fail, we will be exposed for being a fraud or an imposter. Failure is scary because we realize that, deep inside, each of us possesses a desire for something greater. We wonder, "Can we actually achieve greater?" I know for a fact that, yes, you can! I am not promising that you'll be the greatest. Being the greatest at something means approaching perfection—and none of us are perfect. Together, we are on a learning curve that stays with us until the day we die. But we can always reach for something greater and jump into that greater fortune by how we respond and how we handle life's letdowns.

3. **Face the Letdown**

There are times in life when you will have to face a letdown before you are led up to the top. **The letdown is necessary for your growth.** We all have lessons to learn before we can jump up and into our next greater adventure. I know this is difficult to hear, especially when you are going through a period of letdowns. Perhaps the government has let you down. Maybe it's your family and friends. Or maybe it's a romantic relationship that has not gone the way you expected it to go. But, know that worrying about and overly focusing on the letdown is not going to lift you up. It's your faith, trust, and perseverance that will help you jump up.

For example, it is by going through the most trying of times that has helped me develop a sense of patience. Now, I am one of the most impatient people you'll ever meet, but you wouldn't know it if you met me today. That's because I have taught myself to slow down and trust the process . . . although I am still working on this and, sometimes, I have to remind myself to be patient.

I've been blessed with the opportunity to spend lots of time on a farm. I watched the fields being prepared for winter wheat. I watched the planting. And then, seven to eight months later . . . finally! Wheat! Spending time on the farm has helped me to think about how long it takes a seed to germinate and mature into what it was meant to be. Our lives are very much like a small seed—regardless of how big or how small your beginning was, what matters is the potential within you and the greater purpose intended for you.

So, do not despise the small beginnings, the letdowns, or the setbacks—they are part of the growth process to bigger and better things and are necessary for our growth. There are very few shortcuts in this life.

As we've all heard before from Les Brown, Joel Osteen, or T.D. Jakes, "A setback is only a setup for a comeback." And, in my opinion, the larger the setback, the larger the potential comeback.

4. **Brainstorm Your Way Out!**

In Panamá, I spoke to a group of business executives, members of the Panamanian Public Forces, and entrepreneurs. One of the business executives mentioned to me, "Our company has restructured, and we let go of half of our employees—including me. I have no business ideas, and since this is a small country, the opportunities are limited. I'm not sure what to do next."

I asked him what his passion was, and his reply was, "I don't have a passion."

I then asked, "If the circumstances were perfect, and you could be given the opportunity to earn a living doing whatever you wanted to do, what would it be?"

Again, he said, "I simply don't know. I don't have any ideas. I'm not a creative person. I'm stuck. I simply don't know what step to take next."

This was the first day of a five-day conference. We all have ideas. We all have dreams and passions. Many of us have been afraid to share those ideas with others because we have been told, "You don't have the money," or "You are not smart enough," or "You can't do it." And sometimes that fear has paralyzed us to stop dreaming altogether, crushing our passion and vision for ourselves.

I asked the recently unemployed business executive to begin writing down ten new ideas that popped in his head beginning that day. He didn't have to share those ideas with anyone. They could be the silliest of possibilities. But, if you are to write down 10 ideas every day for 365 days, you will come up with 3,650 new ideas every year! I guarantee you that you will have at least one idea that could be patented or lead to an invention that could impact the world in a positive way, or a new business that could change your financial future for the better. The business executive was extremely smart, and he had a bachelor's and a master's degree. By the fifth day of the conference, he came up with a brilliant business idea that is now earning him a greater fortune.

So, what are ten new ideas you can write down right now that could improve the way you do business? What new product or service ideas or business ideas are brewing? Remember that when you are brainstorming, there are no bad ideas. In fact, judging your ideas at this stage will just stop you cold in your tracks.

1. _____

2. _____

3. _____

4. _____

5. _____

6. _____

7. _____

8. _____

9. _____

10. _____

You may even come up with more than ten ideas a day! If you make this a practice every day, you will definitely come up with some cool ideas that will make the world a better place. You have the ability to do more. **Life is about expanding your vision and challenging yourself to jump into the next level.** Writing down a list of ideas daily challenges you to demand more of yourself while you explore your ideas, abilities, and untapped talents. I'm excited to see how you will continue to add value to all of us.

#4

HOW TO HANDLE GETTING FIRED

So, how exactly did I jump out of this scenario I found myself in? I was fired and going from making a great income to zero. I had to start all over again. Below is a list of steps I took to handle the situation. It helped me out, and I believe it can help you, too, if you are ever fired or face a huge letdown in life!

1. **Don't remain bitter.**

   Regardless of how much pain you are feeling, or how unfair the situation is, you must think of the long-term consequences. It's okay to be bitter, but remaining that way long term only causes you more pain internally and does nothing to help the situation. Sometimes you have to walk away, as I mentioned in chapter two. I decided after I was fired that I would not remain bitter. I loved the product I was selling, and I believed in it. What I didn't believe in was the way I was treated. I felt it was unfair. But again, I retained my composure and remained professional. The old cliché of not burning bridges holds true. And I'm very thankful I didn't react from a place of bitterness, or I would not have had the opportunity to purchase the company that fired me.

2. **Don't be afraid to negotiate.**

   You never know how your boss will react unless you ask. They may be willing to help you out, especially if they regret letting you go. Of course, things may not go your way, but nothing is ever lost by asking and attempting to negotiate, even when you feel like you're not holding any cards. (Hey, it's not like they can fire you again!) The worst that will happen is the bosses deny your request or suggestion.

3. **Send a thank-you letter to your employer.**

Yes, you have to be the bigger person, and this is one way to show them that you are bigger! This will earn you more respect and keep the doors open for any future possibilities.

4. **Count your blessings!**

Yes, consider getting fired a blessing. Earlier, I talked about how pain produces power, impossibilities produce possibilities, and the greater the adversity, the greater the advantage. I truly believe this. It's difficult to see in the moment when you lose your job, but you do have things, people, and experiences to be thankful for. Think and reflect on those things. And write them down for those times when bitterness attempts to take over!

5. **Call a hero.**

No, not Superman, Batman, Thor, or any of the fictional superheroes you may be a fan of. I'm talking about what I call everyday heroes. Those are the people in your life who support you and are there for you when times are tough. Your hero could be a family member, a friend, or a coworker. Now, this was not the first time I was fired. I had been fired twice before. The first time I was fired, I worked for one week at a nursing home when I was in my late teens. I was fired because I was told, "You smile too much and nursing homes are for family members who are sick or dying. No one wants to see a cheerful, happy, smiley girl when they enter our building, as it is a sad time for them." The second time I was fired, I briefly had a position selling and marketing testing services to clinicians. The job didn't last long, but I met my friend, father figure, and mentor through this job. I was fired because one of the employees told the company president and vice president that I did "nothing," and they needed to get rid of me because he did all the work. And, since the company did not have a values-based leadership system in place, I lost my job. The individuals who fired me are no longer with the company. (As an aside, gossip is something that we do not tolerate in my company. I am sure this experience contributed to me making a company policy of zero tolerance for gossip.) But the day I was fired, I was so sad. I went to visit my friend Dr. Martin. I said, "I can't believe I was fired! I did so much for this company. I worked extra hours without complaining, and never asked for more pay, despite working weekends and often using my own funds for marketing projects!" He said, "They have no idea what they lost. They obviously don't know how to run a business." He provided the moral support I needed.

He continued, "You are extremely talented, and it is too bad they didn't see it. You will accomplish much more now that you are free to accomplish greater things than you ever imagined. You were simply wasting away your talents with that job. You are too valuable to work there anyway." Dr. Martin believed in me and saw talents I could not see in myself. He was the superhero I needed in that moment!

Often, we only see our weaknesses, and it is difficult to see our strengths. That is why we need to surround ourselves with everyday heroes. So, when balanceback fired me, I naturally called Dr. Martin again. This time I was in tears. I said, "Dr. Martin, I just lost my job. I don't know what to do! Two of my kids have serious medical conditions. I don't have insurance to cover the costs."

He said, "This is the best day of your life!"

"You don't understand," I replied. "It's the worst day! I have no idea how to support my kids. I don't have family to fall back on. I have nothing!"

He said, "You have more than what you need! Now you are ready to start your own company. You are a genius—even I can see it—don't waste time with fools. Use your talents to enrich yourself and your family."

He didn't offer financial support. He didn't offer a job or a handout. But what he provided was much more valuable than any monetary or material gift. I'm so thankful to Dr. Martin for being there for me when times have been so tough, at least in my mind, when I felt these were some of the darkest of days. Who in your life is your everyday hero? Take the time and call or visit them today and thank them for being there for you. And, remember, regardless of how bad you feel your setback is—you, too, can be an everyday hero for someone. So, in addition to calling someone today and thanking them, who will you be a hero to today?

When you don't have the self-confidence you need to move forward, use your hero's words to give you the confidence to carry you through those tough times. I used Dr. Martin's words as a brain vitamin to give me the emotional strength I needed to begin a new project. You can also use the list you wrote of your talents and skills. If you do not have anyone you can reach out to, you can always hire a mentor or coach or attend leadership seminars. You will meet new people, and you will begin to find strong relationships that provide necessary support.

6. **Find your "why."**

At a recent event, my mentor and friend John C. Maxwell asked, "What makes you cry? What makes you laugh?" Sometimes we get stuck with those questions. This is one way to find your "why." Another method I have used to find my passion is to make lists. Make lists of your dream jobs or refer to the lists of ideas you created earlier. Which one fuels you? Which one creates a drive within you? And then uncover your passion. This may just be the door that opens for you to jump through and into your next adventure, as it did for me!

You may need to revisit your lists from time to time, because our "why" may change during different phases in life. When I was younger and a single mom, my drive was caring for my four children. My heart had been torn apart by what they suffered, and I was going to make sure that no one ever laid a hand on them again. My children were my drive to become number one in sales and be the greater version of me. My drive is still my children, but it has expanded now that I have grandchildren! Additionally, I am now eager to serve others through leadership, motivational and inspirational conferences, workshops, and events.

7. **Stand up, stand tall, stand strong.**

When everything around you is crumbling, and you seem to be losing on all sides, stand up. Don't buckle under pressure. I learned that even though I was unfairly let go—I had that truth behind me. Remember to never let someone or a situation determine your value. Only you can do that. When your life is filled with disappointment, failure after failure, and you just seem to have lost all hope, this becomes the time you need to get a grip! Feel your pain, acknowledge it, and own it. Then, and only then, you can stand up and move again.

8. **Let the ball bounce.**

Let the ball bounce where it may. If you have done everything you can in your power to respond professionally and you have remained levelheaded, and you have the determination to succeed, and you know you have done your very best . . . then it's time to let the ball bounce and land where it may.

CHAPTER FIVE

TAKE BIG, BOLD, AND DARING RISKS

In my experience, the best response to a setback is to respond with a big, bold, and daring move. Set the stage for your comeback. Turn every challenge into an opportunity.

Losing my income from balanceback was a big hit to my finances, no doubt about that. I certainly faced some major adversities, but, as you now know I like to say, I believe that **the greater the adversity, the greater the advantage**. Fortunately, I had developed relationships with a few other manufacturing companies, and I quickly won distribution contracts with them.

I needed that income short term, but I had a bigger plan. You might even say it was a big, bold move or maybe even a bit crazy. My friend Nick Vujicic once said to me, "You have to be a little bit *loco*" to go out and do something you've never done before. But I believe that the greater the risk, the greater the reward.

I had become very knowledgeable about the medical device business. I saw how identifying a need and developing a product to serve that need could not only help patients obtain outcome-based results and treatment, but also help clinicians obtain objective data to help them provide better patient care. I created an opportunity to actually *develop* a product that could help clinicians and patients alike. My big, bold move was to go from selling medical devices to creating one!

I had developed good relationships with many top-notch physicians, from family doctors to neurologists to surgeons. On my visits to their offices, I asked them what sort of medical devices they needed but could not find in the marketplace.

I received many responses for different kinds of equipment, but there was one device that seemed to be on the wish lists of many physicians across several specialties—a multi-functional machine that could be used to test the autonomic nervous system, cardiovascular health, and metabolic health, while providing an overall health-risk assessment.

When I took the concept of creating such a machine to medical engineers and research physicians, more than a few said I was crazy. What experience did I have in manufacturing a complicated medical device? Other negative comments included:

Go back to sales. That is what you are good at.

You will never make it in manufacturing.

You don't have the experience, the background, or the funding.

One of my friends who had worked with me in the past said, "Marie, you have no experience in manufacturing. You have no experience in obtaining FDA clearance. But you are good at sales. Create a sales book and a sales course. I will invest in that. But this is too risky."

He added, "Besides, it will cost millions to obtain FDA clearance, and if you get denied, all of the money invested will be a total loss."

I offered him a 50/50 deal, where I would put in the financial investment, and he would put in his expertise. However, during that time period, over 50 percent of the FDA applications were being rejected. The cost to obtain FDA approval, after passing electrical testing, clinical trials, and so on, was astronomical. My friend felt that if we did not receive clearance, all those funds and time would simply be lost, and it would be like throwing money away.

Years later, I met with that friend.

He said, "I could have been a millionaire and owned half of your company!"

I reminded him that he was too afraid to take a risk, and it was his choice to walk away.

In life, there are no guarantees. You can't even guarantee you will survive to see tomorrow. **But, without taking risks, you will never be able to find out just how big the reward potential could be!**

I had substantial income from my other sales clients, but I didn't think my resources were enough to take this bold new idea from a concept to the market. Digging in, I discovered that there were existing off-the-shelf parts and technologies that I could buy without great expense and then assemble for a comprehensive device. I also found an engineer in Europe who could develop the software for me at a reasonable cost. Eventually, to save on manufacturing costs, I allowed him to assemble the shelf parts together for my new device. This also helped to save on overhead, since labor was less expensive where he was located.

In the end, I was able to finance the entire research, development, and testing on my own. This was a tough time financially and emotionally, but the product was going to be capable of providing a diagnostic test for cardiovascular/heart conditions, autonomic disorders, and mental and physical stress. Cardiovascular disorders are one of the leading causes of mortality in the US. But, with my proposed device, screening and diagnostic testing could enable clinicians to properly diagnose and assess risk to help patients avoid heart problems and to improve patient outcomes by providing appropriate treatment, professional support, and assistance in leading a healthier lifestyle to avoid health issues and prevent untimely deaths.

Where people were seeing impossibility, I was seeing possibility. It was too important of a product not to have available for clinicians to be able to provide improved patient care. It was way too important for patients not to have access to such diagnostic screening and testing.

—

I took the plunge and made a commitment to work on receiving clearance to market the device. Such a device could be marketed to primary care as well as internal medicine doctors, cardiologists, endocrinologists, clinics, and hospitals.

Admittedly, the process was not easy. I received rejection after rejection. Not being an engineer, and lacking the engineering background when filling out portions of the application and reports, did not help my prospects. At one point, I was at the brink of giving up! In fact, I thought it was a sign that perhaps I was on the wrong path when I received a call from a company who had heard about my reputation in sales. They wanted me work for them to sell their services in the healthcare industry. I explained to them that I was in the process of obtaining FDA clearance, but that I had just received another rejection letter with deficiencies that I needed to fix.

The company contacting me provided testing for patients who suffered from seizures, to enable those patients to be properly monitored in order to receive appropriate treatment. I would be working with some of the top neurologists in the country. I had already established great relationships with many neurologists who would be needing the service provided by the company. I told them I would submit my corrections and revisions to the FDA, which was about the equivalent of five large packing boxes of paperwork. I told them I would work on this on my own time and would dedicate myself to selling their services. I was running out of money rapidly and needed funds to support myself and continue funding the FDA regulatory costs.

However, I told them that if I received FDA clearance, I would have to quit to work on my company. They agreed to let me work for them even under those circumstances.

Of course, on the first day of training, I received the long-awaited call from the FDA during my lunch break. My device was cleared! I returned from lunch and walked into the training room with the largest smile on my face. I just could not help myself—I started jumping up and down with excitement. They all looked at me and joined in with enthusiasm, and then asked, "What are we so excited about?" I told them I had just received the long-awaited FDA clearance for my product. They were so gracious and kind and allowed me to demonstrate my device to them. They understood that it made no sense to continue with the training since I would be working on my product full-time. They are a great company, and I'm sure if I had not received my FDA clearance, I'd probably be working for them today. The owners of this company are still good friends of mine.

With my FDA clearance, I was ready to roll out the product with a big marketing push to all the doctors, clinics, and hospitals I had come to know over the years.

The name of my start-up was called Critical Health Assessment, and over several years, beginning in 2009, I sold the device to doctors, clinics, and hospitals around the world and turned it into a business doing millions in annual sales!

Because of the steps outlined in this chapter, I was able to see the success of Critical Health Assessment. Soon, after I obtained clearance for the product, I was able to place it in prestigious hospitals, clinics, and universities, including Mayo Clinic and Providence Hospitals. This newfound success got the attention from the owners of balanceback, the very same company that had fired me two years previously.

They called me and asked, "Are you interested in investing in balanceback?"

CHAPTER FIVE
LESSONS AND GUIDES

#1

VISUALIZE

When you have a vision, you do not see how things are. You see them as you want them to be. Great leaders have the knack to see beyond what is in front of them. A good friend of mine is a real estate investor who earns millions of dollars a year by buying broken-down homes and renovating and selling them. Most people who see a home with outdated carpets and outdated kitchens fail to imagine the beautiful hardwood floors where the old carpets lay or the ultra-modern granite countertops in place of the outdated laminate ones in the kitchen.

But, because my friend can, he is able to buy properties at low prices, renovate them according to his vision, and resell at a substantial profit.

In fact, while we're on the topic of real estate, one of the first homes I bought sat on two acres, with a beautiful, wide creek on the side of the home. It was a wonderful colonial-style two-story home built in the late 1970s with a full basement. The problem was that the house still had the original avocado green shag carpet in the living areas, a lot of outdated parquet flooring, and the most hideous gold and silver foil wallpaper you can imagine.

As soon as the realtor opened the door, she took one step in, one step out, shut the door, and told me, "This house is too ugly. I refuse to walk inside that hideous house." She refused my request to view it. So, I called a different realtor, and he took me inside. I was able to visualize how I could remodel and update the home. The structure was solid. The home was custom built by an engineer who had passed away. It was too big for his widow to live in alone, so she wanted to sell it and move into a smaller residence. Since the home was never occupied by anyone but the original owners, the avocado green shag carpet still looked new. The owners never updated the interior of the home, and it had remained on the market for over a year. People would simply walk out as soon as they saw the bright green carpet! I was able to purchase the home for 75 percent less than it would be worth after I updated the interior. The only regret I have on that home was that I did not throw a '70s party before remodeling it!

Learn to visualize, not as in dreaming, but in seeing what isn't there yet. What would your dream home look like if money were not a problem for you? I know that the home I bought became my dream home, not because of what was there when I first saw it, but what it looked like when I visualized it and took action to remodel it.

Visualize where you want to be, not where you are now . . . not where you were in the past. And ask yourself:

"Where do I want to be?"

"Where do I need to be?"

Answering these questions will help you realize your aspirations and give you deeper insight, enabling you to see what needs to be seen to make your vision a reality.

But also, here's an important point of distinction: don't confuse visualizing with automatic success. Often in today's culture, I will hear a speaker say that all we have to do is "visualize" our perfect version of what our world should be. If we don't deviate from that perfect vision, and only think positive thoughts, our lives will be perfect and our worries will go away. In fact, they will even quote scripture to prove their point. Proverbs 29:18 says, "Where there is no vision, the people perish." The speakers often neglect to mention the second part of that verse, which states, "But he that keepeth the law, happy is he." After careful study of other translations, the true meaning is that those who disregard guidance from God will run into chaos.

James 4:13–15 is one of many scripture passages where we are told not to worry about tomorrow, or next year, because we don't know what the future holds. Yet, some leadership "experts" will continue to incorrectly emphasize the idea that we are in full control, and that if any adversity comes our way, it is because we were not thinking 100 percent positively.

I do agree that thinking affects our actions. However, I also know that, in this world, you will encounter challenges, simply because we all possess free will. Some will use their free will to harm others, and sometimes, no matter how positive we are, that harm will be directed toward us or impact us indirectly.

That is why—through my workshops and with my family—I prefer to provide the tools and skill sets you need to face any challenge with confidence, strength, and determination. These tools can enable you to emerge stronger, learning from the difficulties you face and turning them into advantages. I do believe the challenges we face only multiply our strength, confidence, and inner peace, as long as we learn how to respond in the right way.

#2

ELIMINATE FEAR!

I was ready to take a big, bold, and daring risk. But I was scared, too! Fear can cause major distractions that will prevent us from focusing our full attention on our mission. Fear can come in many forms and from the strangest of places. In chapter four, I encouraged you to face the fear. Here, I am showing you how fear presents itself and how you can eliminate it!

1. **Fear of Riches**

    Yes, it may sound odd. But I know many who are afraid of material success. Riches in themselves are not bad; it is when your entire focus is on material success that you lose sight of the important things. And, I believe that is why some Christians are afraid of riches. Many will quote Luke 18:25: "For it is easier for a camel to go through a needle's eye, than it is for a rich man to enter into the Kingdom of God." Therefore, because they fear riches so much, they sabotage themselves from reaching a certain goal. I once found myself in this odd mindset. I was working for a commercial print shop in sales. For some reason, that Bible verse was always on my mind. I would purposely not want to make more money, for fear of being too rich. Because my ex-husband was so jealous of me being in a sales position, it was the perfect excuse to leave that job. Actually, it was necessary to be safe from his jealous wrath, but I have to admit, I was also relieved that I was going to be saved from those "riches" that could keep me from heaven.

Looking back, I realize how silly that thought was. The more successful you are, the more people you can employ. The more people you employ, the more you are contributing to the local economy. And if you grow nationally, or even globally, you are impacting multiple communities, making the world a better place by providing financial stability to many with the jobs you are creating.

2. **Fear of Failure**

My good friend Les Brown often states, "Fear is **F**alse **E**vidence **A**ppearing **R**eal." Now, you have zero evidence that you will fail. Yet, you give power to that fear, without giving yourself a chance. You give up when you are only "three feet from gold" because you are afraid of failure. Instead of trying and persevering, you allow failure to take control. Instead, turn that fear into fuel to guide you toward the truth of your potential—the truth of your passion and determination on how your mission in life is going to make an impact and leave a legacy, not only for you, but for your family, as well as those lives that will be changed with your product, service, or idea that will impact many.

3. **Fear of Criticism**

   Yes, we all want to be liked. But the truth is, there is no way to get 100 percent of people to like you. Why? Because we are all different. Not everyone is at the same level of awareness as you. An old friend called me one day, and said, "Hey, our mutual friend is upset you didn't invite him to be onstage at your event. He is so angry that he said you won't be standing for long because he is coming after you."

   I said, "And you are still friends with this guy?"

   He replied, "Well, you know . . . I just want everyone to like me, and I don't want him to think I had anything to do with you not inviting him to speak on your stage."

   I held an event that cost me thousands of dollars to put together. The arena I rented did not include production costs, lighting, advertising, speakers' fees, and many other costs associated with putting an event together. The individual my "friend" wanted me to include on the speakers list deeply offended me in many ways, which is why I chose not to invite him. To make matters worse, I actually received death threats for not inviting him! And I was saddened that someone who I thought was my friend turned out to care less about my friendship than about being liked by someone "important." But I will take criticism all day long as long as I'm standing up for what is right.

You will face criticism, and that's okay. We can never please all of the people all of the time, and it's always best to work from a set of principles you believe in.

4. **Fear of Incompetence**

    You may fear starting something new because you may think you don't have the skills or expertise. However, today you can hire just about any expert you need to work for you, and information is readily accessible on just about any topic. I am not an engineer or clinician, but I do work with some of the most intelligent engineers and doctors in the world.

5. **Fear of Risk**

    I mention risk more than once, because this is one of the fears that most holds us back! I have a friend who I once offered 100 percent of the profits if she made shirts for an event I was setting up. Now, I had never organized an event before this, and of course, she was hesitant. It was my first rodeo, after all! She asked, "What guarantee do I have that I will make a profit?"

    I said, "There is zero guarantee you will make a profit. In fact, you could lose money."

    Then she said, "Can you guarantee a certain number of tickets will be sold?"

    Again, I said, "No, I can't guarantee that, either. In fact, we could sell tickets and those who buy may decide not to show up."

Her reply was, "If you can't guarantee with 100 percent certainty that I will make a profit, or how many people will show up, then I will not take the risk."

Seven thousand people attended! Would you take the risk to be able to pitch your product or service to seven thousand people and keep 100 percent of the profit? My guess is most of you would. But many would rather not try, unless there had been a guarantee that seven thousand potential customers would show up. But, again, in life, there are no guarantees. If you are not willing to take risks, you will not be there to see the potential reward.

#3

VISION SUPPORT

There will be times when no one else will get your vision. This does not mean you should give up on it. No one could see the possibility in the older home I remodeled. Only after I completed the remodeling did I receive compliments on how beautiful my home was.

Acting on your vision is not always easy. It took me two years of hard work on the development and clinical aspects of our product before I filed the initial application to obtain FDA clearance. My vision required faith, trust, dedication, determination, discipline, and consistency to start a new company without any investors or financial institutions to back me up.

The following steps will guide you toward seeing your vision become a reality:

1. **Surround Yourself with Supportive People**

Like the everyday heroes I mention in chapter four, you need to surround yourself with supportive people. At the same time, you need to eliminate contact with toxic people who will distract you from achieving your goals. I know from experience that sometimes this can be difficult, particularly if you work with toxic people or you have family members who make your life more difficult than it should be. If you are dealing with negative people, you can diffuse the situation by keeping busy. For example, at work, you can state that you need to get your projects done or need to meet whatever deadline you are facing. If at home, you can walk away. If you feel that you simply don't have supporters or encouragers in your life, then take the time to make new friends who are a positive influence. If there is someone you admire at work, you can always ask them if they would mentor you. When I worked for a bank in my early twenties, I looked up to our vice president of accounting. She was always in control. While I witnessed other executives losing their tempers and shouting at their employees, she encouraged her employees. She never lost her temper, even during difficult situations. I used to go into the office early just to learn from her. I read the books she read, and I asked her many questions about business. Fortunately, she was kind enough to share her knowledge with me. Most people who are great leaders want to help others and will be willing to mentor you, because they enjoy seeing others grow, too.

Where can you meet new people? At work, networking events, church, or social gatherings. Always strive to meet friends who are smarter and more successful than you are. It is human nature for us to want to be the smartest one in the room; however, if you are the smartest person, then who are you learning from? You limit your growth potential if you don't surround yourself with those from whom you can learn.

Also, even if you can't rid yourself completely of toxic influences, you can still refuse to let them hold you back. Just remember that you will need to develop wisdom about who you surround yourself with during this time of action. Many may try to demean you or diminish the work you are doing. Often, they do this without realizing that they are taking you off focus. They may think they are saving you from loss by telling you that there is no way you can accomplish your goal, and they will try to advise you to let go of your dreams, your passions, and your desire to get your idea off the ground. It is important for you to surround yourself with people who support you and your mission. Those are the people that will advise you wisely, while helping you reach your goal.

2. **Do It Anyway**

When I served as the marketing department manager for a small bank in my early twenties, I created a concept for a website and presented it to the president. He said, "That is so stupid! No one will ever use the Internet for banking! What a waste of time!" Regardless of his assessment and lack of vision, I took action and completed the website anyway. Little did he know at that time that we would soon be conducting banking not only on the web, but on our phones! Completing the website served me well. The bank was acquired by a larger bank. Because I had built a reputation for my marketing expertise, I was able to do freelance work for other companies, which eventually led to me being recognized by a Fortune 500 company and landing a marketing management position managing a $600 million budget.

3. **Have Patience**

I talked about discouragement in chapter four, but it's worth repeating here. Oftentimes, when we do not see early results, we become discouraged. It took me over two years to obtain FDA clearance on the product I wanted to bring to market. Each time the FDA would send me back my mistakes, I had to work hard to get them all corrected. At one point, one of the FDA engineers responded, "I don't think you will get your clearance. We need more clinical data, and it's going to be tough." Many people would have given up. You have often heard the saying "Soar like the eagle." Eagles have incredible vision, enabling them to see beyond what is considered normal.[1] Eagles are able to catch wind drafts during a storm and fly above it. They rise above the storm. You, too, may experience storms during your path to achieving your dreams. But you were created to see above and beyond the storm. You were created to catch the wind of greatness that lies within you.

4. **Stay Focused on Your Goal**

Now that you have found or discovered your passion, you will need to stay laser focused on your mission. Once you find that passion, you will be able to center your focus. Then everything else will follow.

Your passion will help you develop your mission to get your ideas, service, or product out there. Don't allow power, greed, money, or praise to get in the way of your focus. Any of these can potentially cause "mis-focus." For example, my friend's dad invented a cool gadget for the automotive industry. My friend knew that his dad's invention would transform the way auto mechanics did their job as it was a time-saver that helped reduce mechanical costs to consumers as well.

However, my friend, who was responsible for bringing the invention to market, soon lost focus of the mission and started to "mis-focus" or mis-direct his energies and attention by concentrating on how rich he was going to become and the potential fame that would come with his dad's new invention. Instead of focusing on bringing it to market, he became prematurely absorbed with the fame. He was able to secure interviews, and even appeared on the cover of a magazine touting the invention. He began to spend recklessly.

Sadly, the family experienced delay after delay in getting the product to market. Soon, all the investors pulled out. The product never made it to market. But, a few years later, someone else came out with a similar product that is still available today. My friend and his dad lost the opportunities they once had, because my friend was not able to stay focused and on track to what their original mission was.

Focus requires a lot of faith, trust, and perseverance. This is why you must have passion to keep you going. If you lose the passion, then it will be easier for you to lose focus. For example, maybe you've heard the story "Three Feet from Gold," found in Napoleon Hill's book *Think and Grow Rich*. It's about a young man who quit after months of mining in a Colorado gold mine, because he never reached gold. He sold all his equipment and gave up. The person who bought the equipment became very rich when he discovered gold only three feet from where the previous owner had stopped. Remember, you may face obstacles, and things may get hard. But that's why you need to stay focused! It will propel you forward to not give up until you reach your goal. Distractions will lead you astray, as in the case of my friend. And he was only three feet from the gold.

5. **Don't Focus Solely on the Payoff**
Dreaming of financial success is fine as long as you don't lose your focus! No matter what we do in life, it's never just about serving yourself. When you focus ONLY on what YOU want, you always end up on the losing side. It's not wrong to want to be well off; it's only wrong when you do so at the expense of everything, and everyone, else. I think of the song "Eye of the Tiger" by Survivor. (Yes,

cheesy, but apt here!) Resist the temptation to "trade passion for glory." Fight the fight to keep your dreams alive.

Remember, your passion may be what changes the lives of not only those around you today, but also of those who will follow. In the movie *Lincoln*, when Lincoln was talking about his passion of freeing the slaves, he said, "Not just for the four million but for the generations to come."

#4

MORE ABOUT PASSION

What product or service are you most passionate about? Or, perhaps you are passionate about a sport or hobby you can turn into a business. I have a friend who was a thrill seeker. He decided to turn his thrill-seeking activities, such as skydiving, bungee jumping, and other high-risk hobbies, into a business. He created a club that charged a monthly fee to join him in his adventures. The fee covered any hard costs (such as equipment) plus the time my friend spent scoping out, planning, and escorting members of the club to participate in the activities together. His club became so successful, he franchised it and was able to earn a good living doing what he enjoys doing. More importantly, he is also helping fellow thrill-seekers assemble and "go wild" in a safer environment, thereby helping others get what they want, too.

Perhaps your passion is something altogether different, and much greater—maybe you have an idea that can transform the world into a better place. Harriet Tubman, the American abolitionist, believed in freedom and was passionate about freeing as many people as possible. She went to great lengths to free many slaves—representing thousands of generations who would be born free because of the work she did. Her passion was so great, she was willing to risk losing her life to bring freedom to many. What are you willing to risk your life for? What problems does this world have that keep you up at night? Instead of worrying about the horrors or problems this world is going through, what solutions do you have that could bring transformation? You could be the solution to a real problem this world faces.

Unlike Harriet Tubman, I was not willing to risk my actual life bringing my product to market, but I was certainly passionate enough to improve patient care and help others. Plus, I knew this device could potentially be a lifesaver for the many patients who would now receive an early diagnosis.

Because I was focused on helping others get what they wanted, I was able to put most of my earnings back into the company.

#5

BE MORE DARING

When you visualize big and boldly, you bring into your conscious mind the awareness of what's possible for you.

This makes me think of a friend of mine, Joe Arevalo, who is a successful business owner in various industries. When I met him, I was helping him with his marketing for his freight forwarding company. He asked me, "What do you need to take your business to the next level?"

At the time, I was in my twenties and doing freelance marketing. I still didn't understand the "Think Big" mindset. I said, "Oh, I just need about $5,000 in additional computer equipment."

He said, "NO! Marie, you can't think that way! You need to think BIG! Five K is not thinking BIG."

I didn't quite understand what he meant. To me, $5,000 was just enough. That's not what he was talking about.

Just enough is not enough. Just enough may get you by for the next year or maybe only for this month. You need to visualize big and boldly to help you build something that will have a lasting impact not only on you but those around you and the community you live in.

Visualize big and boldly to be a contributor to society and to leave behind a business, concept, service, or an example that will live on long after you are gone. A legacy that will be carried on by the lives you touch, generation upon generation.

Yes, I'll say it again: the greater the risk, the greater the potential reward! Once you begin the process of big, bold visualization, you then need to jump toward your dream and be daring enough to go after it! The following will help you be more daring:

1. **Stop being afraid of what others may think.**
   When I was a child, I was afraid of what others would think if I sang. So, instead, I lip-synched as I was told to do by my aunt. I later learned that this was foolish, and I forgave myself and my aunt because she didn't know better and I was just a kid. When my now adult son was little, he did not have the musical talent my older kids had.

However, I kept that to myself. When he sang, I encouraged it. He took singing lessons, and when he attended high school in Branson, Missouri, for a brief period, he was often selected to sing solos for the school program.

2. **Take action before you know it all.**

   If you wait until all the stars are aligned, you may never get started. The truth is, you will never know it all. Begin to take action with the knowledge you have and learn along the way. Also, instead of watching a mindless TV show, watch something that will teach you some growth principles to help you achieve your goal. Or, you can read or listen to an audiobook on a specific topic that will help you achieve your goal(s). For example, I read books on marketing, sales, business plans, engineering books, and lots of clinical studies that I knew would help me in the creation of my new business. Although I don't have a degree in business, sales, or marketing, I found that if you really want to learn something, you can buy books on a specific topic. If you can't afford a book, visit your local library and check one out for free. Plus, with today's technology, if you don't like to read, you can watch a YouTube video on just about any topic you want or get an audiobook. Additionally, apps are available for free to read or listen to audiobooks. One I have used that is great is called LibriVox.

3. **Eliminate fear-based thinking.**

   Fear-based thinking does not serve you well. Is there ever a time for fear? Yes, when you are being chased by a tiger.

"FEAR" can be an acronym with a variety of meanings, including "Forget Everything and Run" or "Face Everything and Rise." The choice is yours.

4. **Remain steady.**

Don't lose your equilibrium. Stay focused and balanced. Keep a tight schedule.

I had to get up very early to get work done before taking my kids to school. During school hours, I was working on making sales to save up money for my start-up. When the kids went to bed, I started working. I maintained a consistent tight schedule.

Develop habits that keep you steady. For instance, I formulated the habit of waking up at 4 a.m. daily to accomplish what I needed: creating business plans, budgets, goals, FDA paperwork, and so on. It took me a long time, but this helped me keep a steady pace until I finally reached my goal.

This past Thanksgiving, I developed a bad habit of eating a piece of pie every single day. I told myself I would break the habit after Christmas. After Christmas, I told myself I would break the habit after the New Year. By the time the New Year started, I had gained ten pounds! It didn't happen overnight. It happened gradually. The same holds true in business and in your personal life. You will most likely not reach overnight success, but your consistent habits will either have a negative or positive effect, depending on the habits you choose! I have a personal trainer now, and I work out every day. I realize I won't gain muscle in a day or a week, but eventually I will, and the fat will gradually melt away if I remain steady with the habit of going to the gym every day.

5. **Be passionate about and for others.**

Some of the best ways to find encouragement is to be an encourager yourself. Encourage a friend, your spouse, or family members. Often, we seek encouragement for ourselves and are left discouraged. But when you begin to focus on others—on how you can serve others instead of seeking how you can be served (a lesson my grandpa taught me)—you will reap massive rewards.

For example, I believe you must have a passion for making the world a better place. I was once at a workshop, and someone told me, "I have a goal of making a million dollars this year."

"Great!" I replied. "How do you plan on earning a million dollars?"

She said, "I don't know. It's just my goal to earn a million dollars."

"Why do you want to earn a million dollars? What services or product will you offer to earn a million dollars?" I asked.

Her reply was, "I don't have anything yet to sell or offer, but I do know that I want to be a millionaire."

I immediately sensed a lack of passion in her voice—especially when it came to serving others. Her main concern was earning money. There is nothing wrong with that. However, if you are not willing to serve others to earn a million dollars, it will be very difficult to become a millionaire on that goal alone. The most successful people are passionate about filling a need in the lives of others. The famed Zig Ziglar said, "You will get all you want in life if you help enough other people get what they want." The woman I spoke with that day knew what she wanted for herself, but she hadn't yet figured out how to help others get what they want or need. And, until you figure that out, it will be difficult to accomplish the first part of this vital formula. Your legacy should not be centered around how much you have in your bank account, but the value you contribute to the world.

CHAPTER
SIX

BE BETTER, NOT BITTER

had been managing Critical Health Assessment for about two years when the call came from my former associates at balanceback.

"Marie, since you are doing so well with the new company, we were wondering if you'd be interested in investing in balanceback so we can continue growing, too." The partner on the phone was the same person who had fired me for making too much money.

You can imagine my surprise.

Was I tempted to laugh out loud? Yes, of course!

But I also saw opportunity. I had heard that their sales were down since I'd left. I knew they had to be in the dumps if they were looking for investors.

"I'd have to look at your financials before considering investing," I said.

During this time, a good friend suggested I employ his uncle, who also served as an auditor for the IRS, to conduct a review of balanceback's financials. This deal was too important to just have a regular accountant without direct experience buying and selling businesses. I had met his uncle previously and felt comfortable with him. I scheduled a flight out with him for the review of the company records, financials, and audit to identify the valuation of the company. I hired him as my accountant for a set amount. After a review of the financials, my new accountant said, "Marie, look at sales when you worked for them!"

I looked and said, "Yes, they were high that year."

He replied, "Actually, you made most of their sales!"

After further review, we both noticed that current yearly sales were tanking. I told my accountant, "I don't want to invest in the company. I want to buy it."

———

I began negotiations, by saying, "Your company is worthless. I will give you one dollar."

Of course, I was being facetious, but I wanted to emphasize from the start that without the sales they had when I was there, their company's fortunes had fallen dramatically.

And it worked . . . but not that easily. It was difficult to get all the owners on the same page during the initial stages of the negotiations. But after a lot of drama, I finally bought the company—for a lot less than it was actually worth.

During the signing of the closing documents, Dr. Frank Scarpino said, "Marie, no one will ever disrespect you again."

I asked, "Why? What do you mean by that?"

He replied, "You just bought the company that fired you!"

I hadn't looked at it that way, and we just laughed! After we signed the documents, and we had all of the signatures together, we had one last big meeting with all of the employees. I was a bit nervous, not knowing how they were going to handle having a new owner. I knew some of the engineers from the days when I was in sales. I used to bug them to make changes to the software that I knew would make my clients happier because they were requests made by my customers. So, they had been frustrated with me and vice versa. The reason they were frustrated with me was because I thought software changes were an easy fix. But they were not—the hardest part being the FDA regulations. A software change may take the engineers a few weeks—but the FDA paperwork took three months. On the other hand, they didn't understand why I was so demanding. These all became clear when we began working together.

At that first meeting, I offered every employee shares of the company. They had gone from having ten owners to just me. I wanted them to have some skin in the game because I still needed software changes I knew my clients would appreciate—and I felt that if the employees owned a piece of the company, they would work smarter, harder, and for the best interest of the company!

After the first few meetings, Dr. Frank Scarpino approached me and asked if he could still be a part of the organization. As professor emeritus for the University of Dayton's engineering department, it was an honor that he even asked. He became the chief technology officer. He had led the original engineering team, and I knew no one was a better fit for running the team. He invented technologies for aircraft used in the air force, and continues to work with them on top-secret projects. (Unfortunately, I'm not even allowed to ask about those projects!)

Initially, I traveled back and forth from Texas to Ohio, where the headquarters of balanceback was. I was hoping to move the company to Texas, and I tried to convince the staff to move. But they wouldn't budge. Since the equipment was so specialized, I really was not comfortable bringing on a different engineering team. So, after getting tired of the back-and-forth traveling during my first year of ownership, I moved a second company I had started to Ohio, and began a new life there.

Nine years later, and I'm still living in Ohio—it is truly a beautiful state. And it is always green, unlike Texas, where half the state has that brown, dreary grass . . . unless you water it every day, as my grandfather used to do.

Had I remained bitter for being let go and reacted in kind to the way they had treated me, it would be highly unlikely I would have had the opportunity to buy the company that fired me.

Of course, there were roadblocks along the way. For example, a challenge arose when a foreign vendor who manufactured a small-but-key component for balanceback's main product tried to blackmail me into giving him partial ownership of the company.

Without the component, our product was incomplete. Suing in a different country, with no legal connections, would have cost too much money. Instead, we invested in re-creating the molding and tooling. About halfway into the project, we received a call from the foreign vendor offering to sell us back our molding. After reminding him that we owned it, he agreed to ship it back to us. The cost was about $7,000, but that was far less expensive than the estimated $500,000 to re-create the entire molding and tool set again. We had already spent approximately half that amount in the redevelopment of that component, but we stood our ground, and that was important to me.

I have never met an entrepreneur who experienced success without facing major setbacks and challenges before reaching the finish line. In fact, most of them would rather talk about how they overcame challenges than how they claimed success. Sometimes what you plan does not go your way, and sometimes your plans will veer off into unexpected directions. **Don't be bitter; be better!**

CHAPTER SIX
LESSONS AND GUIDES

#1

SOME THOUGHTS ON FORGIVENESS

Many of us find forgiving very difficult; however, it is key to not allowing the situation to have power over you. Forgiving was the only way I was able to move forward with buying balanceback. Forgiving means a lot, but let me clear up a few misperceptions about the concept.

- You can forgive without letting the person back into your life.
- Forgiveness also does not mean that the offense will be forgotten.
- It does mean that those who wronged you are responsible for the damage and hurt they committed against you.
- Forgiveness does not release the person of the consequences for the wrongs they have perpetuated against you. If the offense is a crime, you have every right to seek justice within the law.

And here's my secret to forgiveness: **Sure, it concerns the other person, but it's actually *about* you. When you forgive, you are choosing to move on. And, even more importantly, you are stripping those who hurt you from having power over your happiness and emotions.**

I know how difficult it is to forgive, especially when the harm done to you creates deep emotional wounds. Every day, I remember the pain I experienced when I discovered the abuse that was committed by my ex-husband against my children. That pain is so deep, there are no words to sufficiently describe it. Introspection and professional guidance on what may be holding you back from being able to forgive will be needed when the hurt you have experienced verges on trauma. Once you identify the reasons, you may be able to take them into account and finally release all the negative emotions and forgive.

Reasons it can be difficult to forgive include:

1. **We want to understand.**

   Sometimes, we try hard to figure out why the person would do such a thing to us. Unfortunately, you may never know the reasons or motivation for their actions. Nonetheless, despite the horrendous ways in which you may have been taken advantage of or abused, the person who committed those crimes doesn't have to explain. That person may just keep doing what they do, and sometimes, there's nothing to gain from trying to understand any further.

2. **Justice is not on your side.**

   There will be times when it feels like bad people are winning and innocent people are being persecuted. It's frustrating to experience this pain. We want to see justice served. But that's not always going to happen. And the more we deny the reality of the situation, the more we (the hurt) suffer. It's not until we look at the possibility in the impossibility that we are able to move forward. My friend Barbara Allen tried to use the judicial system to move forward. When it failed her, she wrote the book *Front Toward Enemy: A Slain Soldier's Widow Details Her Husband's Murder and How Military Courts Allowed the Killer to Escape Justice* and launched her podcast— deciding to let it go and move forward. Today, she speaks to large audiences and makes television appearances on Fox, CNN, and many other networks and radio programs. She is one of the strongest women I know, and I am better as a human simply for the fact that she shared her story on how to turn pain into purpose.

3. **We want to take justice into our own hands.**

   When hurt, you may feel responsibility for bringing down the person who harmed you . . . even to the point of wanting to become a vigilante! One of my favorite novels, *The Count of Monte Cristo*, by Alexandre Dumas, tells the story of Dante, who was falsely accused and imprisoned for many years. Franz d'Epinay, one of the book's characters, says, "Hatred is blind and anger deaf: the one who pours himself a cup of vengeance is likely to drink a bitter draught." At the book's conclusion, after Dante has sought out revenge, he learns that revenge belongs to God and God alone. As a woman of faith, I live by the following verse, from Romans 12:19: "Do not take revenge, my dear friends, but leave room for God's wrath, for it is written: 'It is mine to avenge; I will repay,' says the Lord." If I did some of the things others have done to me, I surely would be terrified to face my God! I remember when my ex-husband was handed a permanent restraining order preventing him from getting near me or my children. This included a permanent restriction from him ever *seeing* any of us ever again. But the order was not good enough for me. I wanted him in jail for the rest of his life. I was living in fear of the possibility that he might harm other children, as well. I finally had to let that go and realize I had no control over how he lived out the rest of his days. I needed to turn my focus toward being thankful that we would never face his wrath, evil actions, and abuse ever again, and to trust that vengeance belonged to God.

Instead of focusing your thoughts on what you want, on how justice should be served, begin to turn that focus around to what you do have. **Focus on the possibilities.** Barbara Allen stopped focusing on how her husband's murderer had gotten away with it and built a successful speaking and coaching business. She stopped focusing on how the justice system had failed her and her family. She stopped focusing on taking revenge. That is hard to do! But as she let go of all these emotions and desires, she started focusing on what she could do. She focused on the possibilities and turned her pain into purpose, inspiring millions of people every day.

And here's more! Scientific studies have shown the benefits of forgiveness. For example, studies have shown that when you forgive, you reap the following benefits:

- You carry less stress.
- You are more self-confident.
- You are more optimistic.
- You are more compassionate.
- You have overall better health with a lower heart rate, fewer chronic illnesses, and lower blood pressure.
- You experience higher cognitive function (the ability to reason, think more clearly, and solve problems more efficiently).
- You receive powerful healing benefits spiritually, physically, and emotionally.[1]

If you have any anger, resentment, or bitterness toward someone, I highly recommend that you say:

"(fill in with the person's name), I forgive you. I no longer hold any resentment or anger toward you. I am free of the emotional and mental stress this situation has brought into my life, and today I choose to let it go. You will no longer have control over my thoughts, my emotions, or my future. I forgive you."

You don't have to tell the person face-to-face, but you can claim forgiveness on your part, agreeing to let go of the hatred, bitterness, and resentment. You will feel much better. You will begin to feel more free, lighter in spirit, and less stressed. Now you can be ready to focus on the possibilities and opportunities that lie in front of you.

#2
SELF-TALK

Often, the difference between a good or bad day is your own attitude. For instance, researchers are now delving into how your own "self-talk," your inner self, can impact you, ranging from eating disorders to sports. A recent study, published in February 2019 by the *Journal of Education and Training Studies*, found that, "Finally, it could be concluded that state sport confidence levels of athletes, a significant psychological factor in their performances, are related with their self-talk level, and one of the important determinants of their state sport confidence levels."[2] Another study published in 2018 found that "rational self-talk [is] more facilitative than the irrational self-talk for putting performance" in amateur golfers.[3] So it is possible to "tee up" for success by being more cognizant of your self-talk and redirecting it to more positive thought processes—it will help you to achieve success much faster. For example, when I trained clinical staff on new equipment, I often heard, "It's going to be too difficult to learn something new!" "We don't have time to implement this."

I would ask them to reframe these thoughts as, "This is a great opportunity to learn something new," or "It's a great opportunity to give our patients more options for their treatment." Plus, having additional experience on your resume is always a good thing. It shows you have the tenacity to tackle new challenges, to continue learning and growing. Once I had the team reframe their mood into a positive state, they were ready for their training.

#3

BE BETTER, NOT BITTER

Building on my thoughts on not remaining bitter in chapter four, instead of being bitter, **show that you are better**! Sometimes what you plan does not always go your way, and sometimes your plans will go in unexpected directions. Don't let your enemies win by turning bitter. Show them you are better instead. Better than any challenge they or any circumstance can throw at you. Better than anger or resentment. Use the powerful energy from your potent emotions (all of them!) to fuel positive growth and to find opportunities. Transform the painful points you will encounter in business or your personal life into passion, and you will come out ahead. Sure, you may have a few bumps and scratches along the way, but you will come out stronger and wiser and with the confidence of knowing that if you survived those obstacles, you can overcome any challenge that comes your way.

Below are steps you can take toward being better instead of being bitter:

1. **Don't be a victim.**

   Yes, I know it is so difficult when you feel you have been trampled on. But being a victim will only encourage you to share your story repeatedly for the sake of seeking sympathy. The sad result only keeps you mired in victimhood status. Instead, you can share your story by simply stating the facts—without expecting any type of sympathy—**with those who can help you**, such as a coach, mentor, counselor, or trusted friend. Conversely, allowing anger and bitterness to take control can result in a feeling of helplessness and a loss of self-confidence.

2. **Stop expecting others to fulfill you or to make you happy.**

   Not a single person on this earth is perfect; even the nicest, most honest person you may know will let you down eventually, because of our human nature. In fact, you will probably let yourself down every now and then. We all make mistakes. But we have to learn from our mistakes without shame and move forward. Instead of expecting others to fulfill your needs, start looking at the good around you. Try to find contentment without relying on others to fill that void. The following suggestions will prove to be helpful:

   Fulfill your own emotional needs. There are several ways you can accomplish this. One is by exercising. Studies show that when you exercise your body produces feel-good endorphins that have a similar effect to morphine, but it's all natural. Secondly, you can build friendships with people who share common interests. Third, take the time to give someone a hug today! Studies show that when you hug someone, your body releases oxytocin, known as the "cuddle hormone," which produces happiness while reducing stress and fulfilling your emotional needs.[4]

Start focusing on what you can do now with what you have. How can you turn your obstacles into opportunity? In early 2016, I had the opportunity to travel to Paraguay with John C. Maxwell, considered to be one of the top leadership gurus in the world according to *Inc.* magazine. We were providing values-based leadership training to government agencies, manufacturing companies, educational institutions, churches, and families using the round table method developed by Global Priority Solutions, Inc. During our stay, we drove by the city's main landfill, where we witnessed one of the most beautiful experiences I have ever seen.

In the middle of one of the poorest, dirtiest, and ugliest places on Earth, we saw the most beautiful smiles, peaceful hearts, and heard the most amazing orchestral music ever played. This orchestra produced the most beautiful sounds, not with expensive instruments, not in lavish concert halls, but outdoors amid garbage, playing instruments made from trash! These children found the treasure in trash, transforming discarded materials into musical instruments. Instead of seeing an old bent-up fork as garbage, they saw a violin tailpiece. And with each piece they selected, they built an entire orchestra filled with cellos, violins, flutes, and many other instruments.

These kids' music has attracted worldwide attention, including the opportunity to tour with Metallica and play their unique instruments with the famous heavy metal band. We were blessed that the children came to our hotel and played selections ranging from The Beatles to classical music. Those children and their families provide a perfect example of turning obstacles into opportunities. And, despite the poverty levels, according to the Gallup 2019 Global Emotions report, the people of Paraguay top the list as having the most positive emotions;[5] as a result, they have been named the happiest nation on Earth.

3. **Learn new skills to propel you to move forward.**

   Perhaps you can start a new business, or you can use your skills to partner with someone to build an enterprise or get a new job where you can use your skills. One day, while on a business trip, I met a young man (he sadly passed away several years ago) whose mother was the founder of one of my favorite Mexican food restaurants in McAllen. His mom opened nine locations before she sold her business to some very successful investors who still run the business today. On the plane, he told me how she had been left a widow with small children. She had no idea how to cook and had never run a restaurant before. He told me how she decided to teach herself how to cook and to eventually open a restaurant to support herself and her family. Her son "taste-tested" all of her recipes and he ended up telling her, "Mom, these are the best tacos ever! People will love them!" Her first restaurant, El Pato, opened in

1974. And in 2020, all nine of the restaurants she started are still as popular as ever. Additionally, according to their website, the new owners have since expanded the business to fourteen locations. The new owners decided to keep all her original recipes. Instead of being mired in sadness from the loss of her husband, she embraced her pain and turned it into purpose. Her philosophy was, "No obstacles, only opportunities."

4. **Accept that it won't be easy.**

    My friend Ken Hartley recently performed an amazing illusion at the GREATER event that I produced (see page 214), taking a newspaper and shredding the paper into many tiny pieces. Then, as his audience gazed in astonishment, he reassembled the shredded pieces, producing an edition that appeared to be hot off the press. He explained that, many times, that is what life is like; it feels as though our lives are being shredded apart. But we shouldn't worry, because everything will come back together again. Ken continued sharing the lessons about life's challenges by reminding us of the movie *A League of Their Own*, about the All-American Girls Professional Baseball League. Dottie, one of the top players, tells her manager, Jimmy, she is going to quit because it just "got too hard." Jimmy responds, "It's supposed to be hard. If it wasn't hard, everyone would do it. The hard is what makes it great." And that is so true.

    So, when times get too hard for you, harness that energy and transform it into your own personal triumph.

In business, you will run into difficult people and challenges. However, if you fuel your energies in the right direction, you can turn those challenges and setbacks into greater opportunities. You can turn assaults and adversities into advantages, disappointments into your destiny, and tragedies into triumph. Yes, as Jimmy said in the movie, "The hard part is what makes it great." Had I not been fired from balanceback, I would have never thought of starting my own company. Being let go allowed me to seize the opportunity for something greater. The greater the setback, the greater the opportunity for a comeback.

Still think making the big jump into something new is going to be easy? Ask yourself these questions:

- Are you willing to risk your security? This may mean giving up a salary if you want to start your own business and quitting your job in order to do so.
- Do you have the financial resources to get started?
- Are you willing to make sacrifices? You may need to give up luxury items or sell some of your material possessions in order to follow your dream of starting your own business.
- Are you willing to take a loss if it doesn't work out?
- Is your family or spouse willing to support you in your endeavors?
- Are you willing to learn new skill sets that you will need to run your own business?

When I started Critical Health Assessment, I had already grown accustomed to eating out often, and always having a full fridge and loaded pantry. To succeed on my own, I had to cut my food expenses and survive on a very tight budget. I eliminated all unnecessary expenses, such as going out to the movies, eating out at steak houses, or buying expensive food items. I needed to make do with ramen noodle soup.

There were no guarantees that I would obtain FDA clearance. And, despite the huge regulatory fees, I was still willing to take that risk. On top of the financial risk, there was the time that was going to be required to put into the new business. I had no engineering or regulatory background experience; those were all skills I needed to learn—at least the lingo—to help me properly prepare the mounds and mounds of paperwork.

It will not be easy. It will be hard. But that's what will make it great!

5. **Beware of get-rich-quick promises.**
Speaking of "accepting that it won't be easy," there are people and companies that may promise you that it *is* easy. I am reminded of multi-level marketing companies who promise you will become a millionaire if you sign up. They sell you on how easy it is and that you really don't have to do anything, except tell two to five of your friends and convince them to enroll as well. Then, all the money will roll in. While I don't have a problem with these companies, I do have a problem with their recruitment methods.

Some of them provide pure hype, without telling you the reality of what it takes to become a million-dollar producer. Although I don't agree with their recruitment strategy, multi-level marketing companies generally provide great products and offer people opportunities to launch their own business without huge overhead expenses. I just believe they must be honest about what it truly takes to make it to the top level.

I remember one company that a good friend of mine convinced me to sign up for. I was not interested in doing the business, but he kept insisting how I would be a millionaire in no time. He introduced me to the top producers in the company. One of them became a good friend of mine. He and his wife were earning $100,000 a month, and they were not visibly working in sales; all earnings were residual. But what they shared with me—and shielded from the public—was the fact that they were laboring eighty hours a week. They worked weekends, late evenings, and early mornings. They reinvested their earnings into massive advertising campaigns, inviting people to "wealth and health" seminars, where they did most of their recruitment. They invested in billboards and radio and television ads. After about ten years of the heavy recruitment efforts, they finally reached millionaire status. Most people don't expend the eighty hours a week, most don't reinvest their money, and most quit the program after the first six months!

A few years ago, I attended a leadership seminar in Toronto, and the leadership guru asked a member of the audience to come up and give a testimony on how they wanted a million-dollar yacht. The speaker said she couldn't afford the purchase initially, but attended the seminar and within a month was able to buy the yacht. The scenario sounded too good to be true, and I knew there was a catch. Hundreds of people signed up for the next level of the leadership program that would provide the necessary skills to reach the same level as the member who gave the testimony. I decided not to sign up, despite the greatly reduced offer that would never be made available again. (It was still a hefty price tag of $15,000, retailing at $25,000.)

During lunch, I asked the member if it was true that she had nothing and within a month she was able to buy the yacht. She said, "Oh, heavens, no! I was already a successful businesswoman. It took me years to save up the money to buy the yacht. In fact, I bought the yacht before I joined this program. They just give me free access to these events if I share my testimony."

Now, I'm not saying that a rags-to-riches purchase of a seven-figure luxury item would be impossible. But more than likely, you will run across challenges.

CHAPTER
SEVEN

EXPECT CHALLENGES

The greater the challenge, the greater the opportunity, right? Well, it may not always seem so, especially when the challenges come from unscrupulous people who think cheating your way to the top is just as good as working for it!

During my years building Critical Health Assessment, just when I thought I had finally found success in my business, a group of toxic competitors crawled out of their caves. Medscore Industries had previously contracted with me to provide distribution for my Critical Health Assessment medical devices. We had sold a substantial number of systems to a large clinic in Dallas that had a group of clinicians working for them. Their patient base was so large, they placed an order for five units at approximately $30,000 each.

The CFO of Medscore Industries called the sales rep who handled the account and requested a meeting with me. I made the trip to Dallas. The CFO said they loved the device and wanted to distribute it under another company name that he owned. He requested that I meet with his business partner, Peter Devin. We scheduled the meeting, and my first reaction was that Devin was not trustworthy. I was not able to pinpoint exactly why, until I accompanied him on a sales call. There, he introduced me to the doctor as his assistant instead of the owner of the company that manufactured the device he was selling!

This experience taught me a valuable lesson: learn to trust your gut. I ignored mine at that time because I labeled everybody I met a "10," giving them the opportunity to shine.

Experience remains a harsh teacher. Unfortunately, I wouldn't learn just how despicable Devin really was for a couple of years. I never truly trusted him, but the CFO of Medscore did business with billion-dollar medical device companies and was highly educated and respected in the community. Because of Devin's association with the CFO, I mistakenly put aside some of my concerns about him.

When Peter Devin realized how successful and profitable my company was, he went to my competitors and offered to join forces with them to undermine Critical Health Assessment. He planned to destroy my reputation, steal my customers, run me out of business, and step in with his own products.

He did this in a way that made it difficult to uncover. Just when I thought I knew how bad the medical industry was, I learned that it was much worse than I had ever imagined or had ever experienced.

$$\smile$$

It started with vicious rumors about me and my company. I wasn't worried about the slander. My company and I had built a solid reputation. But the malicious backstabbing did cause delays in the sales cycles and a blip that made us feel we were back in kindergarten again. The client who told me about some rumors and accusations said that he and his wife (who managed the office) chose to buy from us instead because I still maintained class and didn't stoop down to the competitors' level to trash them.

Trashing your competitors never works! My client's wife said, "Marie, when you presented your product to us, you demonstrated both the features of your product and the competitors'. You even encouraged us to obtain a demonstration from your main competitor before making our decision. You never spoke one ill word about the competition. As soon as we called your competitors and requested a demo, they began to bad-mouth you and attempted to tarnish your personal reputation as well. Because we know you and your family, we knew it was all lies and we could not trust them, which is why we are buying from you."

Still, I had a hard time believing someone would make up such incredible lies. Especially because I had never met a single employee who worked for the competition at that time. The rumors began to circulate to many of my clients and potential clients.

One day I received an email from a distributor of ours who began to have a difficult time closing deals and asked for my assistance. She knew of the rumors and knew exactly how to combat them. But this time, it was different. She was told that we were being sued for patent infringement. I needed to get lawyers involved to stop the rumors because this time the lies were impacting our bottom line.

I asked if the client was willing to provide an affidavit of this so-called rumor. He provided the actual lawsuit. I thought it was fake, since I had never been served and it was dated six months prior, filed in a court far from where I worked and lived.

I sent it to my attorney.

He said, "Marie, this lawsuit is real. You need a patent attorney. The average going rate to hire a good patent attorney is $100,000 a month! If you don't hire an attorney, you automatically lose. And, sometimes if you win, you end up losing anyway. What I mean by that is patent lawsuits are so expensive, and if you are a start-up or a small company, it can put you out of business quick."

And, as I would learn, putting me out of business was Devin's goal. The goal was not to win the suit, but to show the allegations to my customers, hoping they would think the charges were legitimate and stop buying our product. Not only were they trying to destroy my reputation, but to put me out of business so they could take over the market.

I was embarrassed that not only was I being harassed, but so were my customers. I still had not met the competitor. But I knew about them from trade shows, and of course, I would disseminate their brochures along with ours so customers could make informed decisions. I knew they donated significant sums to the American Diabetes Association (ADA), and therefore, they received incredible support from them. My company was a start-up, so I didn't have the resources to donate that kind of money. Neither did I have investors.

The competitor had over eighty investors. Certainly, the CEO was very intelligent. I had learned from the brochures, and his public bio, that he was a 1969 Dickinson College graduate with a Villanova University law degree, a master's degree in taxation, and an MBA in international business from Temple University. I, on the other hand, didn't even have a college education!

I felt that with this man's education, he surely would come to his senses and drop this baseless and senseless lawsuit. But I learned the hard way that just because someone is educated doesn't mean they have values, character, or credibility. Unfortunately, these characteristics, along with trustworthiness, are not mandated degree requirements. I later learned that Robert Welch, the CEO of the competitor filing the lawsuit, had once defrauded a ninety-one-year-old woman of millions of dollars to fund his company. He also had numerous lawsuits filed against him. He lost the suits and owed many people thousands of dollars. But he never paid any of the debt back. After Welch was removed as trustee of the ninety-one-year-old woman's estate, the judge wrote, "The record demonstrates unremitting self-dealing by Robert Welch." He ended up losing his law license for the fraud he committed against the woman.[1]

Regardless, that didn't stop him from being a part of the healthcare industry. Although there are numerous regulations regarding documentation with the FDA, there are no licensure requirements. If you want to sell life insurance, real estate, or even style or cut people's hair, you need a license. But not for medical sales. You can be a convicted felon and go out and sell lifesaving medical devices. There are no legal testing requirements, no courses, no fees to pay. Some companies—like the one I worked for when I got started—do require you to have some knowledge, take a course, and pass a test. But it certainly was not required by any governing agency. Not all companies perform background checks, and not all require potential employees to have any credentials or pass any tests.

Not only was my competitor bullying me, but he was bullying my clients as well.

The situation took a turn for the worse, culminating in Peter Devin filing baseless lawsuits against me on behalf of other people without their knowledge—once they became aware of the lawsuits, they approached the court demanding that the lawsuits be dropped immediately. Sadly, the fictitious lawsuits had already been disseminated to my employees, distributors, clients, and potential clients in an attempt to discredit me and ruin my reputation and my business.

—

Your success can make you a big target. I learned this the hard way when I told my lawyer that I was shocked to be sued.

He said, "Oh, that's normal. The more successful you are, the more lawsuits you can expect. For example, in just one year, Apple faced sixty class action lawsuits, not including lawsuits from vendors, suppliers, and employees."

I encountered some filthy business practices, which is far more common than you might think in the unregulated and lucrative field of medical equipment sales.

In fact, while I was spending more than $2 million on legal fees to fight groundless lawsuits—all of which were thrown out of court—I was also fending off another attack on my company by a Taiwanese software engineer I'd hired to develop my medical devices.

—

In the end, I walked away from Critical Health Assessment. Peter Devin had already severely damaged the company's reputation. This was another example in my life of knowing when to walk away.

CHAPTER SEVEN
LESSONS AND GUIDES

#1
DEALING WITH BAD CHARACTERS

We can learn how to avoid dealing with bad characters and be able to move on ahead with success despite difficulties we may face. To avoid business dealings with unscrupulous people, I recommend that you:

1. **Be a Super Sleuth**
   Obtain a complete and thorough background check from a reputable background check company. Don't rely on online searches. Most recently, a distributor who had just received $500,000 in funding from private investors approached me about distributing our products. He looked sharp. He appeared to have all the credentials, and he was distributing for billion-dollar companies in the medical industry and had contacts and business dealings with people of influence such as politicians, celebrities, and rock stars. Still, I felt there was something not quite

right. I did a background check, and sadly we found that he had been convicted of defrauding investors. This guy's conviction did not show up on the Internet. He had paid a big tech company to clear his name from all searches. However, the background company we hired was able to pull up deleted pages of his conviction with photos and details of his crimes and links to the court documents. Unfortunately, he is still working in the medical device industry, and I fear the $500,000 he received from investors is long gone.

2. **Trust but Verify**

   Generally, unscrupulous people make promises they can't fulfill. For example, salespeople who exaggerate will brag about sales numbers that are typically two to three times more than what top performers produce in the industry. You may be promised to be introduced to people of influence who can help you achieve your goals or gain influence. The businessman who was convicted of fraud bragged about his connections with top politicians and celebrities. He had some of the names on his cell phone, including back and forth text messages he shared between celebrities. Text messages are easy to fake. Because of my previous experience with unprincipled people, I verified his credentials before doing business with him.

3. **Don't Fall for the Flattery**

   Unscrupulous businesspeople will attempt to flatter you in an attempt to lure you with promises of helping you

reach breakthroughs in your industry or to increase profits. I have learned through experience that false flattery
can be very detrimental if you fall for it. During a speaking engagement, a man who was very eager to be known
kept showering me with compliments. I had only recently
met him, and I had a bad vibe about him. I tried to keep
my distance. He began texting me many times throughout the day. If I was at a meeting and did not respond,
he would multiply the number of times he would call. I
registered up to five missed calls from him within an hour.
I thought this behavior was very bizarre. He claimed to be
well connected in the community where we were having
the event, so I felt maybe he was just weird, but not the
type of guy who could cause serious harm. He showed up
at all the community functions, so it was difficult to keep
my distance. Since he was from the same country as one of
my friends, I made the mistake of introducing him to her.
She had flown in from Europe and is a very well-respected
psychiatrist and speaker. Two days after she arrived in the
States—while this guy was sending me flattering text messages on what a great job I was doing with the event—he
was telling her that he could do a better job and saying
many negative things about me. She pulled me aside and
warned me about him. Fortunately, he made the mistake
of texting her some disparaging words on a group text to
both of us. He immediately deleted the message, but not
before I was able to get a screenshot of it.

4. Differentiate Between Education and Wisdom

Being able to differentiate between education and wisdom will also carry you far. I have learned that just because someone is educated, it does not mean they have wisdom. Most of you can recognize wisdom in others. The traits of wisdom include virtue, honesty, sincerity, humility, and empathy, just to give a few. The best lessons I learned in life came from my dropout grandparents. My grandfather had a third-grade education, and my grandmother had a first-grade education. My grandpa had to drop out of school due to the Great Depression. My grandfather's parents owned a small chain of grocery stores along the Rio Grande Valley from Harlingen, Texas, to Mission, Texas. When the Depression hit, they were forced to close their stores and take up any work they could find—which was out in the fields picking cotton. My grandmother also had to quit school to help out at her family farm, in Beaumont, Texas, picking strawberries. They both taught themselves to read and write.

They were both humble business owners. My grandfather had a barbershop right next to my grandmother's beauty salon. Many dismissed my grandparents because of their lack of education, but the most valuable nuggets of wisdom in business and life I ever received came from my them.

For example, it was my grandfather who taught me the value of forgiveness. He would say, "Vengeance is not yours; it belongs to God. Instead, forgive."

Had I not followed this one piece of advice, I would never have become CEO of the company that fired me.

Another piece of wisdom I use in business is a principle they taught me: "The more you give, the more you receive."

My grandfather would give a free comic book to every boy who got a haircut. He had a magazine rack where kids could choose anything from Spider-Man to the Archie comic books. Growing up, I spent lots of time in the back of his barbershop reading Casper the Ghost, Richie Rich, and many of the Marvel comics.

My grandmother always had fresh-baked breads and cookies she made from scratch, coffee, water, sodas, and small snacks available for all her clients while they waited for their hair to get done. After their service was complete, she would give them a small gift (usually hand lotion or a shampoo/conditioner set) as a token of her appreciation. I picked up on those lessons. I'm there to serve my customers. They are not there to serve me. I've often provided free marketing or consulting services before anyone buys from me—and I continue the relationship, by adding value, after the sale is made. A principle I learned from my grandma that helped me become number one in sales.

And, most importantly, I gained a lot of life's most valuable lessons from how they lived their lives—they provided an example of what true leadership looks like by making an impact on everyone they made contact with. I remember my grandma picking up her broom to sweep the work stations of her employees. She would often buy her employees breakfast and lunch, showing me the value of humility, kindness, and compassion as a business owner. Even the local drunk would get a daily free meal from my grandma. She didn't want to give him money because she knew he'd use it to get drunk—but she always bought him food.

My grandparents taught me that how you choose determines your success. Instead of judging the drunk, she showed kindness. Instead of vengeance, they showed forgiveness. Instead of asking to be served, they served. Instead of fear, faith. Wisdom may come to you from places you never expected. Look to the unlikeliest places and you may just find wisdom there.

#2

DEALING WITH A TOXIC SITUATION, A CASE STUDY

One of the competitors who I introduced you to in this chapter once left me a voicemail saying, "You are an orphan; you should have never been born; your mom was mentally insane—you worthless *****," along with other inappropriate and derogatory comments. I realized he was insanely jealous of the impact we were making in the community through our GREATER events (see page 214). Evidently, he also heard part of my life story. Following are some of the steps that I used to handle this toxic situation.

1. **Accept your situation.**

   Yes, my mom had a mental illness, due to brain damage.
   Yes, I did not know who my father was. He was not present in my life. However, these circumstances *did not* and
   do not define who I am, nor characterize my potential.

2. **Recognize any feelings of anger, resentment, and the
   need for revenge and let them go.**

   Romans 12:19: "Avenge not yourselves . . . for it is written,
   Vengeance is mine; I will repay, saith the Lord."

3. **Take responsibility for your actions.**

   I was beginning to internalize the competitor's ugly words,
   and they impacted the way I was responding to others. I
   was in a consistent horrible mood, and when a friend who
   was trying to be helpful suggested that I call the police,
   I snapped, "The police won't do anything! They don't
   care!" I had my reasons for saying this, but, that's a story
   for another day.

   My tone was harsh, and that was not an appropriate
   response or action to take. I was allowing anger, a vindic-
   tive attitude, and hatred to take control. I quickly recognized my behavior when my friend put her arm on my
   shoulder to let me know that she was only trying to help.
   I did call the police, but they said they could do nothing
   because the name or number appeared as "unknown" on
   the voicemail; nor was there a name left with the voicemail. Les Brown, considered by many as the number-one
   motivational speaker in the world, was with me at that

time and also heard the voicemail. Fortunately, he was there for me to offer emotional support.

#3

DEALING WITH A TOXIC INDIVIDUAL, A CASE STUDY

On another occasion, a toxic individual who was trying hard to get involved with the GREATER project made sure to show up at most of my meetings, including a dinner meeting. During this dinner, the chief medical officer of one of the hospitals asked me several questions, including how I came up with the concept of the event. The toxic gate-crasher rudely interrupted, not allowing me to answer the question, and said, "Look, she just got lucky. No one knows her and she will not succeed. I'm the famous one; I am president of . . . ," and he proceeded to list all the organizations he claimed to be president of.

"That every braggart shall be found an ass," wrote Shakespeare. Need I say more? I must admit my emotions were getting the best of me. I kept thinking, "Who does he think he is? Why is he so rude and condescending?"

But, before I jumped the gun, I managed to get a grip on my feelings.

I realized that when two people confronting each other are unable to control their emotions, disaster is sure to follow.

The best approach is to:

1. **Take your thoughts captive.**

   When you are insulted, it is natural to feel upset. But remember, you are still responsible for how you react to the situation. Once you recognize your emotions, you can begin to take control of your thoughts and responses. Do not take things personally, even if what someone says to you is true, such as the time I was left a message stating that my mom was "mentally insane." When someone says something to be hurtful, it is generally because they want to tear you down through their jealousy. By taking you down, they wrongly think they lift themselves up. However, when you take someone down, you go down together.

   Once you take control of your thoughts, you can focus on remaining calm. If you act angry, scream, or take physical action, you risk agitating the person further, raising the threat of increased harassment.

   If you remain calm, the person doing the bullying will likely stop, because he is no longer getting a reaction from you. If you are unable to stay calm, walk away until you regain control of your emotions.

   During my confrontation with the uninvited "expert," the CMO cut him off, looked directly toward me, and said, "I want to hear from you." Again, the man kept interrupting. I simply paused and then the CMO took charge, saying, "Please, stop interrupting her. I have heard enough from you—let her speak." The man's rudeness to me now extended to everyone at the table. Not only did everyone recognize his actions, but he also lost respect when he was put in his place by someone else. Had I lost my temper or stooped to his level, BOTH of us would have lost respect.

2. **Talk to the person with respect and courtesy.**

Tell that individual how his/her words made you feel. For example, I once heard a coworker, Julie, tell another female coworker, Jackie, "Why are you wearing that dress? The color is not a good color on you, and you don't have the figure for that dress."

Julie then told the other ladies in the breakroom, "Jackie looks too good, and I'm jealous of her cute clothes. I told her that the dress didn't look good on her so that she doesn't get a 'big head.'"

Jackie was standing outside the breakroom close enough to overhear part of the conversation. Confronting Julie, Jackie asked, "Why would you say that to me? I just heard what you said in the breakroom." Julie apologized profusely and never made another negative comment to Jackie again.

3. **Laugh it off!**

I was at a conference in Dallas with my boss and a group of executives, business owners, and sales representatives. I was the only woman and the only minority. I was also recognized as the number-one sales representative in the country. My boss was asked, "Where did you find her? She is a great sales rep." My boss said, "I taught her everything she knows. She is a fast learner. If I hadn't given her the opportunity, she would be cleaning houses right now, or begging for food by the border, where we found her with her four kids."

Although his comments were insulting and degrading, I turned his words around and made a joke out of it. I said, "Yes, I'm up to minimum wage now, and now my kids and I all have new clothes."

After that, the insults stopped, and we just laughed it off.

4. **Change the topic of the conversation.**

During a business meeting, my boss said, "Why do Hispanic people call themselves 'Latino' or 'Latina'? That is so stupid; there is no country called 'Latin.'"

Well, I have never called myself a Latina, as it is not a term used where I grew up, and I had no idea where he was coming from or why he'd made that comment. However, I did know why the term was used in other parts of the United States. I had to give him a lesson in history, but since we were in a meeting, I didn't have time for a long discussion, so I changed the topic back to sales, the purpose of the meeting. When the meeting ended, I explained that nations located in Central America and South America are considered part of "Latin America," because the languages spoken there are influenced by Latin more than other languages. Therefore, people from South America/Latin America often are referred to as "Latina" or "Latino."

#4

BE CONSISTENT

Consistency gave me a leg up when vicious rumors began spreading about me and my new company. In business, you need consistency to quantify how you spend your time. Additionally, it's necessary in order to measure your progress or regression. You will need a minimum of six months of consistency to measure success in a given area. Consistency helps you maintain:

1. **Accountability**

   When you implement consistency in the workplace or in your professional life, you establish accountability. People depend on you. You become accountable by objectively measuring your progress toward your success.

2. **Reputation**

   Your consistent tactics help you develop a reputation you can be proud of. In business, if you are constantly changing your logo, your customers may get confused and wonder if you are a new company. Or, if your marketing message is constantly changing, it will be difficult to maintain, measure, or manage your reputation. Your message to either your family, friends, or business associates remains constant when you maintain consistency. It eliminates the guessing game of where you stand. I remember my mom promising to pick me up after school. Because of her brain damage, she often forgot to pick me up. However, as a child, I did not understand that very well. Therefore, I always felt insecure not knowing if she would pick me up that day or if I would end up waiting at the school playground until dark.

It is important for your friends, family, and business associates to know they can trust you and your word. To know that when you say something, you mean it. This is especially true in raising your children. I raised four children single-handedly because their dad lost parental rights. Consistency is a principle that helped me guide my children into successful adulthood. My "yes" always meant yes, and my "no" always meant no. I had a fifth child at the age of forty—he is now nine years old. The other day, my nine-year-old was not doing a good job of listening, and I had to redirect his behavior in front of my oldest son, who is now twenty-seven. My oldest son said, "You better listen to your mom because she means what she says and she always follows through. One time she grounded me from Xbox for an entire year!" My nine-year-old is normally a very well-behaved boy, so he was shocked to learn how long I grounded my oldest son from the Xbox. He asked his older brother, "What did you do?" Eliminating Xbox privileges turned out to be the best decision I ever made for him. My oldest son had become addicted to gaming. It was impacting his school-work, and he would sneak out of his room to go play the game in the living room in the middle of the night. When

I grounded him from the Xbox, he developed an interest in music and today he is a successful music producer. Consistency matters in all aspects of your life. You will gain the respect from all who know you.

However, beware of being so consistent that you become compliant. Consistency is important for gauging what works and what does not work, but action is also required—by being consistent on your actions. Consistency in setting goals without taking action is not going to help you, those around you, or your coworkers. Remember also to gauge your progress. Merely exercising consistent compliance can be counterproductive.

#5

SHIFT YOUR FOCUS TO SERVING INSTEAD OF HOW YOU CAN BE SERVED

During business dealings, I concentrated my efforts on being the best we could possibly be, providing exceptional customer service, clinical training by the top clinicians in the world within our field, and improving on our products to have the most advanced technological systems on the market. Therefore, I spent little time focusing on competition. I knew what they offered and would simply let our clients decide what product was most convenient for their practice by showing a comparison and asking them to request a demonstration from us and the competitor before they decided to purchase.

Overwhelmingly, and I would say 99 percent of the time, when a client obtained a demonstration from us and the competitor, they chose our product. There is a saying in sales, "She is so good at sales, she could sell ice to an Eskimo." This means you are so good at convincing people to buy from you, they will even purchase products they don't need. My conscience would never allow me to sell something to someone that they couldn't use or that would not add value to them. Often, when I have been approached by a manufacturer to sell their product, I say "no" if I don't believe in the product. One of my good friends has been trying to get me to join his multi-level marketing company for over fifteen years. I still have not signed up for it. He believes in the product. I also believe it is a good product. However, I can't use a multivitamin kit that includes some the size of horse pills. To placate him, I agreed to order a year's worth of those vitamins. I took them to work and offered them to my employees, but they didn't want to take them, either. I had to throw them out because they expired.

Therefore, because I believe in representing the top-of-the-line products, I have always encouraged my clients to test other products as well as ours before purchasing. I believe that when you have the client's best interest at heart, they will appreciate your selflessness. Sales is about adding value to others. It's about providing something someone needs to make his or her life easier. Because medical device sales can be very lucrative, I've seen salespeople focus on their own financial reward while totally disregarding and disrespecting their clients. When I first started, the company gave me a list of names I could sell to. I mentioned one of the executives who had given me the names to the customer, hoping to provide common ground that someone they trusted and purchased from referred me.

Almost every person on that list told me how upset they were that they bought from him. I was embarrassed that I worked with an organization that had someone on the team who had a total disregard for others. The complaints included stories such as this: "He sold us this $35,000 piece of equipment and promised to do the installation and training. He was a great sales guy. But he simply dropped off the machine and never trained us. He didn't even put the equipment together for us as he had promised."

To make things right, I decided to provide the training at my own expense, even though I was not the one who sold the equipment, but they were now my customers and I was there to serve. I felt bad that the customers had been treated so poorly. I approached the executive and asked him, "Why would you sell an expensive piece of equipment and then leave the customer hanging?"

His reply was, "Marie, in business you have to be shrewd. Think about it. Once someone spends $35,000, they are not going to buy another one. You must move on. Time is money. It's no big deal—you will never see the customer again. But they are buyers, and that is why I gave you the list of names, so you can sell them the new product we carry." I was initially disgusted with his attitude, but then elated, as a short time later the company president fired him.

When my customers saw that I was adding value before they even made a purchase with me, I gained their trust. I became more of a consultant, and then they began to purchase products from me. That approach is one of the reasons I climbed to the top national sales position within that organization. Many of my clients have become good friends; we vacation together with our families and we stay connected.

I have a friend in insurance sales, and he would grow frustrated when the company he represented failed to provide the insurance product his clients truly needed. Eventually, he quit and started his own company representing multiple insurance companies. This allowed him to provide his clients with the product that worked best for them, not the product that would give him the highest commission payout. His insurance colleagues thought this was a crazy idea, because in some cases, he could have sold a policy that would double his commission. However, my friend believes in creating lifetime relationships. Because he values others first, he puts in place products that benefit his customer and not his pocketbook. As a result, he has doubled his client base. Although sometimes his commissions may be smaller, at the end of the year, his income is much greater because of a doubled client base. Plus, he does not have to work so hard, as most of his clients come from referrals from his existing clients.

We developed a winning combination through the process of putting the interest of others first, including those of my clients and potential customers; by avoiding negative/derogative comments about our competitors; and always focusing on how we could compete against ourselves instead of others. Following these principles allowed us to focus on making our products and services better than if we focused on what the competitors were doing.

We used an ethical, successful process that made all of us greater.

#6

NEGATIVE DIDACTICS

Wouldn't it be nice if everything in the world was positive? Imagine a world where you never encounter any negativity. A world where everyone was nice, cheerful, enthusiastic, and nothing ever went wrong. Well, that's not the case! There are always things right there, ready to get us down about ourselves and our abilities.

I call these negative didactics, because we always have the opportunity to learn from them. And when we learn from our negative experiences, we grow. It is often said that we learn from our mistakes or from someone else's. I know I'd rather learn from someone else's mistakes than my own. Unfortunately, sometimes God has to hit me over the head with a two-by-four to get it. Here are some mistakes I have made, which hopefully will provide an example for you so you don't have to go through them.

1. **I've often focused on life's challenges and failed to recognize my potential.**

    For example, after I built a successful business and bought the company that fired me, I was hit with that baseless patent infringement lawsuit. I had no idea about the lawsuit until I learned it had been disseminated to all of my clients and potential clients six months earlier.

Focusing on my problem and challenges during the rough two years it took to resolve the case caused intense emotional stress and began to impact my business.

The truth was, I felt inadequate to handle the situation and I began to focus on those inadequacies. I had temporary amnesia and had forgotten my grandmother's lessons on faith and trust to know that, YES, I was capable of handling the situation. Remember, YOU are fully capable of any challenge that comes your way! You may feel inadequate at times, but you are able!

But I failed to see my potential and strength and allowed fear to set in. I had to recognize that no one could steal my soul, because I know who I belong to. I had to remember how difficult it was to even be born! There is a purpose for my life, and there is a purpose for your life as well. Don't allow others to steal your joy, your peace, your gift, or your potential. You were created for something much bigger and greater. The world deserves the gift of your talents.

Because I was so focused on fear and my perceived inadequacies, I was temporarily blinded to my potential and my gifts, and was not able to properly focus on my company's strengths.

2. **Negativity is contagious.**

A study found that negativity truly is contagious. People are more likely to be swayed toward negativity in a group setting, according to the research.[2,3] I recently hosted a very successful motivation event, with seven thousand people attending. One attendee was very negative. He complained that there were simply too many speakers. The event was designed to have highly impactful speakers, who each spoke for no more than twelve to thirteen minutes, much like a TED Talk. However, these were solely inspirational and motivational messages. The man said, "What could you possibly learn in such a short time?"

Evidently, he had never heard of a TED Talk before, where much wisdom is shared in thirteen minutes or less. In fact, I learned that for forty-five-plus years of my life I was tying my shoes the wrong way, causing them to become untied much quicker from a popular TED Talk; but now they never untie, until I untie them myself. The program showed us how to tie our shoes properly. You may have seen that video, too—as it is one of the most popular TED Talks!

The few people who were with this attendee all said, "There were too many speakers who didn't speak long enough," almost repeating the negative man's words verbatim. The majority of the audience, however, seated nowhere near the negative man, asked for the dates of the next event because they could not wait to attend the following year. We received tons of emails, phone calls, and invitations not only to bring the show back to the same community but also to locations worldwide! What I learned was that it is best to squash negativity as soon as possible, or it can destroy your team, just as a rotten apple causes the rest of the bunch to spoil faster.

Fortunately, happiness may also be contagious! The well-known Framingham Heart Study,[4] which has been used to study health, emotional, and social networks since 1948, found that during stark economic times, people offered $5,000 in cash would be only 2 percent happier than being a friend of someone who spreads happiness. Because, as research shows, happy people tend to spread their cheerfulness like a virus, making you happy, too!

What I have learned is to surround myself with happy people. Sometimes in life, though, we have to work and live with those who are more like Eeyore from *Winnie-the-Pooh*. Like Eeyore, nothing could ever seem to make them happy; they tend to look at the thorn on the rose stem, while ignoring the beautiful rose with its lovely fragrance. When a negative coworker approaches me to share some gloomy news, I generally will state that I must get back to work and I don't give into the gloomy conversations. You, too, can set limits on how much time you want to spend with a negative coworker or family member. If you have a family member who is often trying to engage you in a confrontation, you can choose to simply walk away. You will maintain your dignity and respect in the long run.

EIGHT

CHANGE ... COUNT ON IT

Learn to adapt to change and welcome the opportunities it presents.

The one thing you can count on is change. Just when you think you are master of your universe, along comes some major shift that throws your planet into another orbit. Don't fight change. Count on it. Be flexible, creative, and even eager to adapt and thrive. Without change, life would be boring!

Rather than get mired in international lawsuits while fighting to salvage a business with a damaged reputation, I shut down Critical Health Assessment. This was a tough decision because it also impacted my employees. I offered them positions within balanceback and helped others transition into new careers. For example, one of my employees would ride the bus to work. I knew it would be difficult for him to find a new job, so I gave him a car, helped him brush up his resume, and trained him on how to ace an interview.

Studies have shown that when people lose a job, or face some type of crisis, they often experience depression, anxiety, and low self-esteem. Knowing this, it was important for me to find resources for my employees. If you find yourself facing an unsurmountable crisis, please seek support from family and friends, and don't be afraid to reach out to a professional to help you bounce back. It may be the perfect opportunity for something new and better for your life. I think of my everyday hero mentioned in chapter four, who told me getting fired was the best day of my life. I didn't see it that way immediately. I was full of panic not knowing how I would care for my children's healthcare needs. But because of his encouraging words, I was able to pick myself back up and find new opportunities.

They say that in this world you are born a winner or you are born a loser. I don't believe that for a minute. My perspective is that we only have choosers. You can choose to win by the choices you make. How you choose to react to adversity, trauma, or even blessings in your life determines your character. And, as my friend Nick Vujicic says, "Attitude is Altitude"—your attitude will affect how far you will go in life. So, at the end of the day, your choice determines your character, your attitude, and your altitude.

Our team members who shifted over to balanceback chose to focus on winning by developing new products and improving every aspect of balanceback.

$$\sim$$

When I bought the company that had fired me even though I was its top salesperson, many of my competitors and detractors said, "Not only will she bankrupt balanceback, but she will be bankrupt herself within six months."

It was meant as an insult, but I used it as motivation. And if you've learned nothing else about me from this book, you know that I consider myself fortunate that we had to walk away from Critical Health Assessment. We chose to win. And my team of clinicians and engineers were then free to create a superior product that is now patent pending. Had we kept Critical Health Assessment, we would not have thought of opportunities to develop a product that does more, is more efficient, more accurate, and provides outcome-based results for clinicians.

Although the entire experience was an emotional and financial nightmare, it proved that the greater the challenge, the greater the opportunity! You need to force yourself to jump into opportunities when faced with those challenges instead of jumping backward and allowing obstacles to break your spirit. Remember, it's your choice. It's not something you were born with.

Not that we didn't have our challenges! Just as I took over balanceback, which is a high-end medical device manufacturing company that was responsible for manufacturing, distribution, and sales, the market began to melt away. Our market was clinicians, because only they can diagnose and treat. Meanwhile, the number of patients suffering from conditions our devices diagnose and treat continued to grow. In a trend that has continued to this day, our primary customer base, general practice physicians, began selling their practices to large hospitals. Changes in the healthcare industry and economic pressures were forcing them to do this.

Managing a medical device manufacturing company requires a lot of capital in order to keep high-level employees, purchase equipment, and maintain governmental regulations. So, we had to get creative.

In addition to serving our military, another step we took was to shift our focus to sell our devices to hospitals. To counter the loss of private practice physicians, we targeted hospitals across the country, including those at major medical schools and universities. Today, hospitals at Yale, Dartmouth, and Vanderbilt, just to name a few, use our equipment.

Still, there were far fewer hospitals than private practices. My challenge was to use my creativity to adjust to the changing market. I had to find and develop new customers for our devices, and I did that by expanding our sales internationally.

Over the last decade, I have led our company as we have overcome major regulatory challenges and built relationships with sales distribution networks around the world. Today, you can find balanceback devices in nearly every hospital in Hong Kong and throughout Asia, India, Europe, South America, and Canada.

My experience in business has taught me that, regardless of your situation, how you choose will determine your altitude.

We have survived and thrived, but no entrepreneur can afford to rest on her laurels, and, believe me, I haven't. Most industries will go through change, and in order to thrive during a transition, you must be willing to think outside the norms and embrace change.

CHAPTER EIGHT
LESSONS AND GUIDES

#1

EMBRACING CHANGE

The following tips will help you when you face changes in your industry—whether they come from regulatory changes, changing trends, the economy, staffing, or suppliers.

1. **Engagement**

   Because I made it a priority to engage my employees in every aspect of our business, we were prepared to handle the changing trends in our industry. **Employee engagement results in loyalty, honesty, increased productivity, and lower employee turnover.**

   For example, during one of our early brainstorming sessions, I asked each employee to jot down their goals and then share how we could collectively help each other to achieve them. Many employers are afraid to invest in their employees or to help them achieve their goals. This is a huge mistake. If you invest in your employees, you will have a staff who is honored to work with you, and those are the type of employees you want!

One of our technical engineers said, "My goal is to travel the world." To help him meet his goal, we send him on installation assignments to doctors' offices across the nation and internationally. He usually books the installations on a Friday or Monday so that he can have the weekend to explore the city he is visiting. And he is a much happier employee working for a company that has helped him achieve his goal.

As we have come to know him more and become more engaged with our staff, we've found out he absolutely loves Disney. He has an annual pass to the Disney complex in Florida and has traveled to every Disney park, including those in Tokyo and Hong Kong.

I was disheartened to learn that he had received a job offer with Disney, but happy when he refused it. I asked him how he could resist such an offer. He said, "Because with Disney, I would not be able to travel. Here, I am able to travel all over the world and live my dream as a world traveler."

I encourage you to discover the answers to these questions:

- What motivates your team members?
- What are the likes/dislikes of your team?
- What are their goals?

- What do they find challenging?
- Who inspires them?

There is so much to learn from your staff that can help you give them what they want, and, in return, they will help you build your successful business.

2. **Embrace Technological Change**

Too many business owners are afraid of new technology. Learn how to harness the new technological advances to benefit your business.

For example, with the advent of AI (artificial intelligence), we were able to incorporate a video professor into our system so that clinicians can access clinical support at any time. A logic tree showed clinicians exactly how the results were determined for verification, automated voice commands, and instant access to our clinical staff, just to name a few of the over thirty new enhancements that were added since I bought the company. I won't mention all of them here because of the clinical lingo, but we could write an entirely new book just on this one topic!

3. **Always Have a Backup Plan**

When I bought balanceback, a supplier attempted to blackmail me, but we had a backup plan and did not fall into his trap. The medical device industry is challenging because we simply can't replace one part with another without going through mounds and mounds of FDA paperwork. Generally, it takes a team of experts in quality control, clinicians for validation and testing, and engineers about six months to make small software changes. Hardware changes could require a year or more to complete. Now, when we develop a product, we test various parts. We process paperwork for multiple parts, so if one supplier is no longer able to supply us with the parts we need, we have an alternate solution without creating a delay in our ability to deliver or to jeopardize our profitability.

4. **Surround Yourself with People Smarter Than You**

    If you are an employer, you want to hire people possessing skill sets your team is lacking. If you are an employee and want to jump ahead in your organization, the same holds true. Surround yourself with people who are smarter than you and have strengths in areas in which you are weak. When I worked for a Fortune 500 company, I would seek out employees who were more skilled than I was in certain areas. I recall my counterpart in another department saying, "If you keep on hiring people smarter than you, you are going to lose your job, because they will take over your position!" My response was simple. "Our department went from a $1 million deficit to a $1 million dollar profit center. This would not have happened without 'smart' employees, who were stronger in certain areas than I was. If I hire employees lacking in the same areas I lack in and possess skill sets weaker than the ones I possess, we would still be a department with a $1 million dollar deficit." Her reply was, "I never thought of it that way."

Unfortunately, too many people operate out of fear: the fear of losing their position, title, or job altogether to someone who is more talented, skilled, or educated. If you focus on the growth of your business and employees, you will leave fear where it belongs—back in the dark closet, never to be touched again.

After five years with that company, I acquired five additional departments, turning each one into a profit center.

In your personal life, you also want to surround yourself with people smarter than you; that is the only way you will continue to grow and thrive. I'm not saying you cannot have friends of different intellectual levels—that's great, too—because you can be a mentor and role model for others. But you also want to make sure that you are always growing. You can't continue to grow if all the people around you are at a lower level of awareness than you are. You will simply limit yourself to where you are without growing any further, thereby capping your potential.

5. **Invest in Yourself, Your Employees, and Others**

Always provide learning opportunities and growth opportunities. I guarantee you that as your team grows, so will your business! If you are an employee, invest in yourself, and you, too, will grow in your relationships and career.

I was consulting a million-dollar medical practice that was already successful, but they had much room to grow and could easily take their practice from $1 million a year to $50 million. I have personally seen and helped single-practitioner practices with three employees grow into multi-specialty groups with over a thousand employees. As I advised the CEO/Clinical Director, he said, "No! Then my secretary is going to leave me if she learns new skill sets! And I will end up wasting my money so that someone else can benefit from my investment in her!"

This type of thinking stems from a scarcity- or fear-based mindset. I'm still a bit shocked to see such highly educated individuals who operate under this type of thinking. This type of mindset holds them and their businesses back, preventing economic and personal growth.

Investing in your employees is a proven strategy. Published studies show that employees value, trust, and remain loyal to employers who invest in them.

For example, Hansson[1] conducted a study on approximately 5,900 private companies in 26 different countries. The study concluded that the "economic benefits" of training outweigh the cost of staff financial turnover. Additionally, Bassi et al.[2] likewise identified a "relationship between investment in training and total returns for shareholders in a sampling of U.S. companies." Numerous studies from countries worldwide report a sharp increase in company profits through factors such as employee satisfaction, education, and skills attributed to training.

By investing in your employees, you will gain:

Employee Satisfaction. Studies indicate that employees who receive training are more efficient, have a greater sense of responsibility, are more creative and motivated, and have a higher sense of job satisfaction.[3]

Increase in Productivity. Surveys conducted in US companies showed an increase of up to 12.7 percent in productivity.[4] Furthermore, investing in employee training reduces defective work by up to 7 percent in a study with 157 US companies.[5]

Increased loyalty. Employee training often results in loyalty to the company who took the time to invest in the employees' growth. Employees who need to seek training outside their business do not feel as connected to the company they work for and are more likely to leave.[6]

The same holds true for your personal life. The more you do for others, the more fulfilled you will become in your own life. An interesting study was conducted by researchers at Stanford. They found that people who were seeking happiness tended to be more depressed, because they were looking at their own emotional happiness and would seek to fulfill it through careless spending, friends, or anything that helped them feel "happy" in the moment. Basically, their emotions were driving them—their emotions of seeking "happiness." But when people looked for ways to serve others and invest in them, they found that they were much happier, in the sense that they were emotionally stable, had more contentment, and were better equipped to handle life's challenges. In other words, when they were not seeking their own happiness, their world didn't fall apart. They could handle challenges in stride because their lives were not based on their own emotions, but instead on investing in others.

6. **Set Specific Goals**

When providing your employees with a project to complete, rather than simply saying, "We must finish this project," you need to be specific. Instead, say, "We need to finalize the project by (certain date). Completing the project by (specified date) will allow the company to add another value-added service to the clients we serve." The following are example targets your employees would have specific details about:

- Productivity Target
- Financial Target
- ROI (Return on Investment) Target
- Other targets pertaining to your organization

Follow up with regular meetings. Once you set goals for your employees, you will see immediate results. I recall that I had an employer who asked me to fire an employee soon after I was hired. The employer said the employee was simply lazy and never finished anything. I asked the employer to give me thirty days to work with this person. If there was no change, I would fire him. We sat down for a one-on-one meeting and created some goals. We evaluated the goals on a weekly basis. Every week, this employee not only completed all the assigned work but went above and beyond the expectations that were set in place, resulting in a higher end-of-year bonus.

However, always be prepared for times when things don't go as planned. Sometimes we set goals, but due to unforeseen circumstances, our goals do not come out as planned. When we are emotionally and mentally prepared to set goals and make plans but understand that situations beyond our control may cause a delay, change, or disruption, we will still be OK. For instance, in our organization, we have had goals set in place, then suddenly a drastic change occurs in which we need to readjust our goals and strategy. In one instance, we were preparing for our yearly ISO 13485, which is an International Standard for Medical Devices. Right about the time we were about to complete it, the laptop models we used for our proprietary software were discontinued. Windows announced they would no longer support the current software with the new one they were developing. The changes are not too complicated. However, when it comes to regulatory requirements, those changes require between three to six months of paperwork. Therefore, you should always have a Plan B at the ready when setting up your goals, and be prepared mentally and emotionally for the unexpected. I have watched executives lose their temper when something out of their control impacts the plans they have set for their team or company. Losing control helps no one and lowers morale. Often, the reason they lose control is because they had no secondary plan in place and they became overwhelmed with the challenges. When you have a secondary plan in place, it helps establish a sense of calm, knowing that there is another route you can take to accomplish your goal without frantically trying to find a last-minute solution.

7. **Make Honesty a Habit**

On a personal basis, we lie to protect ourselves, avoid trouble, and mislead others. We lie for the same reasons and more in business. I always start with the laziest reason not to lie: once you tell one lie, you usually have to not only tell more lies, but you also have to keep up with the previous lies. A habit of lying can get you frazzled, and you have to rely on a good memory to keep your story straight. When you tell the truth, you don't need such a good memory! When you or your organization walks a trail of lies, you get so accustomed to it that it becomes a part of you. Eventually, you become known as a pathological liar. Have you ever known someone who lied even when they didn't need to? Lying has become such a habit that they can't operate without it. Lying has become a part of who they are. Lying compounds problems you are trying to hide or cover up because you begin to add lies on top of lies. I recommend recognizing the magnitude of the consequences resulting from lies in the workplace and make a clear policy that lying will not be tolerated. Make honesty a habit, even if you risk losing _____ (fill in the blank). Recently, a client of mine was having problems with a manufacturer (unrelated to our business). Because I had a good relationship with the doctor, he reached out to me and asked for my advice. The manufacturer illegally logged onto their computer, disabling their system. When the doctor called to have it restored, they said, "You need to pay $10,000 for an upgrade to get it to work." They violated HIPAA regulations by accessing his computer with patient data without explicit permission from him or his patients. In addition, they resorted to extortion to try to get more money from him. When he told them he was going to report them, the manufacturer said, "We didn't sell you the equipment, and you can't prove it because you bought it from a distributor, not directly from us." The hardware that was connected to the software had the manufacturer's name all over it. They are now under investigation.

8. **Focus on Results**

I was conducting a site visit for my client Jack Myrna in Texas earlier this year. Jack had approximately 1,200 employees. He was an extrovert and loved people, so he tended to build "friendships" with the employees that were most like him. One particular employee would invite Jack out for drinks once a week, usually on the weekends. Jack enjoyed going out and relaxing with his employee, talking about family, kids, and work. Unfortunately, this employee's results were causing significant financial loss to the company. In fact, the results were so poor, other employees were taking notice. The morale of the entire office declined significantly. Jack found it difficult to fire his friend, and instead gave him another chance to improve job performance. But by this point, the employee grew distrustful of Jack and began operating out of fear. The employee took actions that hurt Jack and his company. For example, he would do his best to demean Jack by sharing with other employees those private conversations they had when they went out drinking. He also tried to find fault with Jack, and brought it to the other employees' attention, attempting to build a case against his boss in the event Jack would decide to fire him. Eventually, the employee was fired. However, by that time, Jack had suffered a huge financial loss amounting to thousands of dollars. While you may enjoy the company of some employees over others, the key is to always stay focused on RESULTS, not personality, friendships, or identifying favorites.

9. **Lead by Listening**

Take the time to listen to your employees' ideas and thoughts on how they could bring value to your business. You may not agree with them, but some of the best ideas may come from your employees. Ask for their feedback. Keep them abreast of your goals and vision for the company. The more you share with your employees, the more they will feel like they belong and are part of your goals and vision, too.

10. **Power Up**

Elevate your employees' self-esteem and sense of value by acknowledging their work and contribution to their departments or projects. When you can acknowledge someone's work and say, "Jonathan, you did a great job!" this immediately "powers up" your employee and motivates him to do more, helps him feel appreciated and valued. Similarly, if a mistake has occurred, take responsibility for it. Your employees will know you have their back, and they will appreciate the trust you have in them.

How do you react if your employee screws up, causing the loss of a big account? Discuss the issue with the employee privately. Do not discuss it with anyone else. Did your employee resolve a difficult situation? If so, make sure you let your employee know you appreciate their conflict resolution skills.

#2

NEVER COMPARTMENTALIZE

Compartmentalization has consequences.

When I came back to balanceback, I found that the previous owners had compartmentalized all the departments, effectively turning them against each other, causing serious dissention.

Engineering felt they were the smartest, and without them, there would be no company.

The clinicians felt they were so gifted that they didn't need to involve any other department in their decisions, projects, or ideas for the growth of the company.

The accounting department had become so separated, they had no idea what any other department was doing.

My first year of ownership was tough, particularly trying to bring cohesiveness to the various departments. Accounting could not understand why they needed to know what was going on in sales. Our engineering team could not figure out why we needed to form a new sales staff. No one in the company had any respect for sales, since the previous owners would regularly put down the salespeople before eventually firing them. What they failed to understand was that it was the sales staff that kept the company's profits coming in!

The sales team also needed to understand the importance of the engineering team. After retraining all of the departments, and introducing new Key Performance Indicators (KPIs, to be discussed in a later chapter), I was finally able to bring all the departments together and help them feel like they were part of the same team. But it was not easy! I recall one day when I requested the financials from the head of the accounting department. She flew off the handle and said she had never been requested financials so frequently! Before I purchased the company, there were ten owners and several investors. The owners would spend the investors' money, and there was no accountability! This resulted in a financial disaster, which allowed me the opportunity to buy it up when their sales shrank due to poor management and lack of performance. Yes, it does require a certain aptitude to succeed in sales!

Every one of your departments and each employee is important, from your landscaper and janitor to your highest-paid executive. Let them know they have value, as they all play an integral role in the success of your business. Do not compartmentalize, but work on the cohesiveness of your team.

#3

SHARE THE VISION

My good friend Dr. Michael DiBlasi, a cardiologist, decided he wanted to do more than prescribe pharmacological treatments and provide surgeries for his patients. He began offering free classes on how to reduce the risk of a stroke, heart attack, and diabetes, and his practice doubled in size. Most importantly, his passion and love for his patients transcended to his entire staff, allowing his staff to be part of the solution for Dr. DiBlasi's patients. Why? Because he shared his vision with his staff to help his patients reverse diabetes, prevent chronic illness, and avoid unnecessary surgeries.

His staff was able to rally around Dr. DiBlasi and joined in his concept of helping the community live healthy lives. My friend worked late and came into the office early to do research and find ways to improve the overall health of his patients. He successfully reversed diabetes for numerous patients.

One afternoon, Dr. DiBlasi invited me to lunch at the local Chili's in his small community, and it was one of the most beautiful experiences I have ever had at a restaurant! An older retired couple came up to our table and thanked Dr. DiBlasi profusely for what he had done in their lives. They looked so healthy and vibrant and were sharing with us how they enjoy dancing every week again—just as they used to when they were a young couple. They had dearly missed this activity during the period before they met Dr. DiBlasi, as one of them was diagnosed with diabetes and diabetic peripheral neuropathy, making walking, much less dancing, excruciatingly painful. The other spouse suffered from a heart condition and had difficulty breathing. To hear how their lives were transformed and how they were enjoying life again was a beautifully moving experience!

Soon, many people started to come over to the table to greet Dr. DiBlasi, thanking him for the new energy they had in their lives, and how they were so thankful for his generosity in helping them restore their health. I had tears of joy in my eyes, and I was also so thankful for the many people Dr. DiBlasi helped in his clinic. I felt as though I was with a celebrity, and in a sense, I was, because he was one in his community.

I have had the pleasure of meeting all of Dr. DiBlasi's employees. I can see that the qualities in my friend are passed on to his employees, and they all share the same working DNA.

Share your vision with your employees, and they will feel inspired and motivated to be part of the big picture you all can share together to grow your business.

#4

VALUED EMPLOYEES ARE LOYAL

Let your employees know you value them. Studies show that when you value your employees, they are loyal, achieve more, and have a higher sense of satisfaction with their jobs.

You can help your employees feel "at home" and part of a "family" by remembering their birthdays and sending cards for weddings, anniversaries, and other special events in their lives.

Employees are the backbone of your company; the more they feel valued, the more they will give back to your company in extraordinary ways.

Do something fun for your employees, like providing a summer company picnic outside the office. When I worked for the financial institution, in addition to the marketing, I was also placed in charge of organizing special events for employees. We had great summer picnics, with fun activities, like having sumo wrestling contests. We outfitted our employees with sumo wrestling outfits that were outrageously huge—it was hard to walk in them when you had them on—but it was so much fun to watch the employees get in the ring. One year we hired a hypnotist, who successfully hypnotized our CEO to believe he was a dog. He literally barked and ran around the room on all fours, acting like a real dog. It was all in fun. The fact that the CEO was willing to "play" and participate with all the employees—and not be afraid to look silly or feel that participating was beneath him—endeared him to the employees and created a bond with them.

During my employment there, I went through a devastating divorce from a marriage marred with frequent abuse. One evening I was beaten so badly that my face was black and blue. I could not afford to miss work, so I did my best to cover my black eye and bruises with makeup. Unfortunately, my best efforts did not cover up my bruises.

The CEO noticed my bruises and asked me to come into his office. I did not want to share my personal problems with him, but he helped me feel at ease and assisted me in getting the help

I needed to get out of the precarious situation I was in. He provided resources and support, and he handed me an envelope with cash to help me pay for legal expenses.

During the divorce proceedings, I received death threats by my ex-spouse, which warranted a restraining order. The CEO notified the employees that if they saw him near the premises to call the police. The CEO helped me feel truly valued, appreciated, and part of the family.

As a CEO, business owner, or manager, showing personal interest in your employees will go a long way toward developing loyalty, dependability, and trust. This usually results in higher productivity and reciprocation.

Although I received numerous job offers, often with higher pay, I remained loyal to my boss and the company I worked for because the little things my boss did counted at the heart level. I stayed with that company until they were sold to another company.

A good friend of mine has been with her employer for ten years. Although she often receives job offers with higher pay, she refuses to leave her current employer. I asked her why she is so loyal. She said she feels like part of the family, and it would be very difficult for her to leave her boss.

"What does your boss do that makes you feel part of the family?" I asked. She said, "My boss always brings me Starbucks in the morning. She buys me gifts for Christmas and my birthday; and when my son was born, she threw a baby shower for me." Although none of those gifts can replace the salary she would receive working for another employer, it is the small gestures, the treatment she receives as a "family member," that keeps her loyal to her employer.

As stated in the beginning of this chapter, the one thing you can count on is change. Just when you think you are master of your universe, along comes some major shift in the way things were that throws your planet into another orbit. Don't fight change. Count on it. Be flexible, creative, and even eager to adapt and thrive. Without change, life would be boring!

NINE

TURN YOUR WEAKNESS INTO A SUPERPOWER

Due to my success as an entrepreneur, I have been invited to speak on international platforms to share with others some of the essential lessons I have learned. As a result of speaking internationally, I have met some of the most inspirational and motivational speakers in the world.

At one of these events in Los Angeles, I had the privilege of meeting my friend Nick Vujicic—considered the number-one inspirational speaker in the world. We had a great connection and decided to work together on a project. The project would soon be called GREATER. And on September 28, 2019, I launched the GREATER series of motivational and inspirational events.

The first one was held at the Bert Ogden Arena in Edinburg, Texas, a new facility that seats 7,500. During the first event, which we set up like an inspirational variety show, we partnered with a local school district to incorporate an anti-bullying program. The program provides personal and professional development skills to enable young people to be fully equipped with the skill sets to jump toward success. Other speakers joined me, including: Nick; Raymond Orta, a rising star in the comedy world (he kept his performance rated G for the kids, but it was seriously the funniest performance I'd ever seen!); Barbara Allen, founder of *American Snippets*, one of the top patriotic podcasts in the nation; the illusionist Ken Hartley, who taught leadership lessons as he performed his act; and many other top speakers. The orchestra we invited played an inspirational piece from my son's classical composition, while professional dancers, who had practiced for six months, performed their beautiful choreographed dance routine. We also had professional singers from Europe perform.

The idea was to use the funds from the event to invest in the youth of the community where the event was held. The day after the big event, Nick and I spoke to 13,000 students, and had the event livestreamed throughout the United States at various schools. We had over 480 school districts who were livestreaming the event to their classrooms and auditoriums. Additionally, we were able to implement a Values Based Leadership Program, which resulted in a 91 percent success rate at an at-risk school district.

We certainly encountered numerous challenges along the way, but regardless, we delivered an amazing program to thousands. We realized a huge success in the outreach to inner-city schools, proving once again that, although a situation may appear grim, there is always greater fortune waiting if you simply look at the opportunity instead of the obstacle. We are continuing to expand the program to reach participants throughout the world. The goal is to provide transformational, intellectual, and emotional growth strategies so that those who attend can unleash their greater selves and build their greatest possible lives.

The reason I got involved in speaking internationally, with speakers such as John C. Maxwell, Nick Vujicic, Les Brown, Bryan Tracy, and many other well-known motivational speakers, is because I have been asked to share how I was able to lift myself up as a single mom who was fired and then ultimately bought the company that fired me. Public speaking allows me to give back to others who are facing similar challenges from domestic abuse, inspiring them to pursue and develop a successful career in business.

My involvement in GREATER doesn't mean I have slowed down in my other career. Every entrepreneur and business owner must be ready, willing, and able to adjust to changing regulations, technology, competition, and markets. I've done that with my bounce-back company, balanceback, by expanding our customer base domestically and internationally.

⌒

Know that while you may feel discouraged at times, there is greater fortune awaiting you.

You can unleash greater fortunes when you tap into all of your talents, potential, skills, and unique gifts. Begin your greater life now.

You are unique. You have skill sets that are unique to you, talents that are unique to you. Every single one of us is the same in that we all face challenges. Yet, we are different in that we each have unique qualities unlike anyone else's.

For instance, I'm often told I am unassuming. Sometimes this could be seen as a weakness. But I use this uniqueness as an advantage. I've seen some women who try to be as authoritative or as intimidating as a man in order to gain greater respect in the workplace. I use my unassuming nature naturally. I don't try to hide it, I don't try to change it, and I don't try to impose a different aura that I know I don't naturally have.

During negotiations, most people put up walls, defenses, or protective barriers in an effort to gain the advantage. But people simply don't do that with me. They see me as an unassuming, easygoing, "can't hurt a fly" type of person. This often results in me being bullied, or attempts are made to take advantage of me. Mostly, however, it results in people placing so much trust in me that the walls, defenses, and protective barriers are never put up, allowing me to negotiate on a level playing field.

Earlier this year, I spoke to a group of female executives in the financial industry. I was asked, "How do you compete against a man?"

My reply was, "You don't."

They said, "What do you mean? You work in a male-dominated industry. You made it to the top. How did you manage that without competing against men?"

I said, "When I started in the industry, I was told by a sales guy that I could never outsell him because he could take the doctors hunting to his ranch, fishing, and to strip clubs."

He was right, too. I had no interest in fishing, hunting, or going to a strip club. But I didn't have to. He used his skills in selling by schmoozing, and I used my unassuming manner to get the deal closed. We were both top producers. He used his skills and I used mine. I didn't have to try to be him or use the talents he had. And I never had to go to a strip club to close a deal!

During the early years of selling medical devices, I was at a business conference. One of the ladies there told me that she had got a "boob job," or breast enhancement, in order to help her boost her career. She told me that I dressed too conservatively and it would hurt my career. She offered to take me shopping to show me how to dress "sexy." Being "sexy" is just not my thing. Growing up, I hated to wear dresses. I preferred jeans. As an adult, I prefer business suits rather than short skirts, halter tops, or mid-drifts. Being sexy is her thing, but I'm simply not gifted in that way. I'd rather be me and stick to my conservative way of dressing. However, I do love super-high heels, but that's because I'm so short and I like to stand a little taller. So, she may have closed deals with her short skirts and showing off her curvy body, but I closed deals by being me. And you can close deals by being you. Of course, there are certain values and strategies that you must follow to be successful long term, which I teach in my sales training seminars.

I recall talking to one of my physician clients, Dr. Castrillon in Florida. We were on break during a training seminar for the use of $85,000 of equipment I had sold to him. I had heard from all my male counterparts how I was not going to make it in the industry, yet Dr. Castrillon was one of the several physicians I closed during my first three months on the job. I asked, "Dr. Castrillon, would you prefer to buy from a female or a male when purchasing capital equipment?" He said, "As a matter of fact, a male." I asked, "Why?" He said, "Because females generally just come to the office to take us out to lunch; they don't know much." I responded, "Then why did you buy from me?" He replied, "Because I didn't expect you to know much, but you knew what you were talking about. It was a no-brainer to buy from you; you had the knowledge, which is rare."

Obviously, I know he is wrong in that regard, because I know many women who are very smart and men who are not too bright. There are both smart men and women, just as there are both men and women who are not too bright! The prevailing mentality that men are intellectually superior to women causes some females to not even try. But I used this flawed perception to my advantage. Dr. Castrillon did not expect me to close a sale with him because I'm a woman. He didn't lay down the barriers. He was open for me to make my presentation, although he may have thought, "What does she know? This can't take too long." When he realized that I knew what I was talking about, I was able to make the sale.

CHAPTER NINE
LESSONS AND GUIDES

#1
THE VICTIM CARD

Another important step you must take very seriously is to eliminate the "victim" mentality. I touched on this in chapter six, but I want to tease this out a bit more.

I used to believe that I was worthless growing up because I was a "bastard child" and my mother was mentally disabled. I was a failure in school. I received straight Ds, barely passing, and I barely graduated high school. Since no one seemed to care, I didn't care, either. I thought I was in a hopeless situation because I was not going to make it to college. I was doomed to a life of misery, poverty, and destruction; or so I thought.

When I became pregnant with my first son, I realized I could not make excuses. I had to grow up. I had a new life to care for. I didn't have a college education, but I could make up for a lack of formal education by becoming the best employee at my workplace. With the impending arrival of my son, I knew there was no longer room or time for excuses, such as, "I barely passed high school," "I'm poor," "I am a bastard child," "My mom is mentally ill," or "My life is nothing but a series of unfortunate events." I needed to eliminate that "stinkin' thinkin'" and take personal responsibility for this new life coming into the world.

#2

CONTINUE THRIVING

No matter what obstacles life presents, you can continue to survive and thrive amid your challenges. Here are a few suggestions.

1. **Make a List of All Your Past Challenges and How You Are Still Here**

   Yes, you are okay. You survived. You made it through. You will make it through again. I remember all of the challenges launching my very first event and thinking, "Why did I choose an arena? I should have started small!" I didn't think I'd make it. But then I remembered my roots lie in Texas. I'm a Texas girl, and in Texas we do things Big. Yes, it's true! Everything in Texas is bigger—except for me—but I have a big spirit and I remembered all the things I had already survived and overcome. Surely, we would get through this challenge, and we did! Go ahead and create a list of everything you have overcome. Let it serve as a testament against the judging voices that pop up every now and then as well as the external voices that want to tear you down.

2. **Have a Purpose**

   My purpose with GREATER was to impact as many students as possible. During our first event, we impacted 35,000 at-risk inner-city kids! Sure, we didn't make a profit. But we had a purpose, and because we had a solid purpose to help others, we reached our goal with an amazing success rate with the program we implemented.

3. **Believe in Your Skill Sets, Strengths, and Abilities**

   I still remember sitting in Dr. Martin's office crying, saying, "I can't believe I was fired!" and his reply, "This is the best day of your life!"

   Yes, sometimes a kick in the butt is the best form of medicine for you, as it was for me! Look at adversity as a means to make you stronger. Remember the baseball adage from *A League of Their Own*: "It's the hard that makes it great." The adversities, obstacles, and challenges in life will only make you stronger and wiser. And you already have everything you need within you to face adversity.

4. **Accept Responsibility**

   Take ownership and responsibility for your mistakes. Then let them go. Wallowing in guilt will only hold you down. Accept that you've made some mistakes, then release them and move on. Not accepting responsibility and blaming others will keep you ten steps behind. Accept your part in it and move on.

5. **Keep on Going**

   Don't allow your past adversities to take hold of you. If you focus on your losses, it will be harder for you to recover and bounce back. Instead, ask yourself the hard questions: "What can I learn from my mistakes?" "What can I do better?" "What can I do to avoid making the same mistake again?" "Am I prepared to take the next step?" "What options do I have?" and "What are the possibilities?" Looking back will only keep you back. You need to keep going and don't stop until you make it to the top. And one of the best ways to keep going is to learn from your past, by asking the hard questions, preparing you for your next big move upward.

6. **Let Adversity Be Your Window of Opportunity**

Adversities, problems, and challenges are what lead the world of innovation. When there is a problem, inventors come up with ideas and solutions to solve it. In the same way, when you are faced with adversity, a window of opportunity has been created for you to consider an option or possibility you may have otherwise missed. Had I not been fired, I would have never looked at owning my own business. I was happy as a sales representative, but it wasn't until I was fired—and with the help of some of my "hero" friends—that I was able to see through the window of opportunity of becoming an entrepreneur.

7. **Simulate Potential Problems**

In my business, we are required to have a quality control department. It is responsible for having CAPAS (Corrective and Preventive Actions) in place—a Food and Drug Administration (FDA) requirement that must be part of our Quality Control Manual and Standard

Operating Procedures. We need to consistently monitor our procedures to determine when and where to take corrective action to improve the process and correct any errors or potential problems.

During my first year of running balanceback, I discovered the hard way the importance of CAPAS during one of our mandatory audits. When the auditor asked for our CAPAS, I said that we did not have any. He said, "You should have a minimum of five CAPAS every year." I replied, "But nothing is broken—we have nothing to correct." He said, "Everything can be improved, and if you don't have CAPAS, that means you are not measuring the progress of the systems you have in place. This time it is a warning, but next time, if we don't see any CAPAS, you will get written up."

Sometimes the auditors do not check for CAPAS, but we learned our lesson. We have CAPAS in place, forcing us to always think of creative ways to improve our processes and systems. We maintain consistency, allowing us to track our progress and determine where improvements could be made.

We also try to re-create potential problems—even though they don't currently exist. This gives us the training and strength we need to face those problems if they do appear.

I recently saw the movie *Midway* and was reminded of how important the process of preparing for potential problems is. In the movie, Lieutenant Richard "Dick"

Best is shown flying a plane as if it is going down—with the motor dying out, the wings down, you name it, while making everyone extremely nervous, especially Chief Aviation Radioman James Murray. Dick responds by saying that you must practice and prepare for the worst-case scenarios in order to make sure you survive the toughest part of the battle.

During a videonystamography test (VNG), considered the gold standard for diagnosing dizziness, balance, and central nervous system disorders, this is exactly what we try to do.[1,2] We re-create dizziness so that we can identify the problem and find out what is causing the dizziness. Fortunately, the dizziness re-created during the test is minor and most patients do very well, as it is a noninvasive test—it just makes the patient's eyes a little "googly" during the procedure, which lasts about thirty seconds at most. (Our company specializes in manufacturing the iVNG equipment!)

In life you will face battles. How prepared are you when you face problems that haven't been encountered yet?

#3

NOTES ON HUMILITY

There is a saying that you should never praise yourself—instead, praise should come from others, not your own lips. Nor should you claim a place in the presence of great men; rather, it is better if they ask you to "come here" than for you to humiliate yourself in front of them by insisting on seeking the best seat and then being told to move because that was not your rightful place. The Bible warns often about arrogance.

"Do not exalt yourself in the king's presence, and do not claim a place among his great men; it is better for him to say to you, 'Come up here,' than for him to humiliate you before his nobles" (Proverbs 25:6–7).

"Let someone else praise you, and not your own mouth; an outsider, and not your own lips" (Proverbs 27:2).

"But when you are invited, take the lowest place, so that when your host comes, he will say to you, 'Friend, move up to a better place.' Then you will be honored in the presence of all the other guests" (Luke 14:10).

Leading in humility, rather than in pride—in trying to seek your own honor—will prove more beneficial for you. Those benefits include:

1. **Freedom from Attempting to Achieve Power and Fame That Continually Seem to Elude You**
   When you are truly modest, and let others take the seat in front of the room—you are free to be yourself. The stress of trying to be "first" will be released from you, giving you peace of mind.

2. **Being Viewed as a True Leader**
   Show that leaders who have a humble spirit are more respected, trusted, and have more influence. True leaders look at how others contribute; they don't try to demean others to lift themselves up. Instead, they shift the focus off themselves and place it on the contributions of others.

According to some of the world's notable individuals, effective leadership also means providing strategy and direction to others, inspiring creativity, empowering others, and sharing the credit.

Wise leaders serve their teams by sharing their knowledge, respect of others, integrity, and humility, while leading with values-based servant leadership—it's one of the most important leadership lessons if you want your business to succeed. Most businesspeople have heard the term "servant leadership." Numerous studies have proven that servant leadership reduces employee turnover, improves productivity, and increases employee satisfaction, among other benefits.[3]

Servant leadership does not mean that you act below your employees. It does not mean that you allow yourself to be bullied. But it does mean that you will not bully others and you will help your employees grow in their careers, treat them with respect, and lead with humility. In the Bible there's a story about Jesus in the book of Luke that resonates here. He tells his disciples that the greatest will become the least and the leaders are those who serve, and then he makes a powerful statement: "I am among you as he that serveth." This was a shocking statement coming from a culture where the religious leaders sought to take the best seat, sought to be served, and sought to be acknowledged. Now that is some powerful leadership.

3. Making Deeper Connections

Humility enables you to admit when you are wrong, or when you make mistakes. All of us make mistakes. All of us are wrong at times. But when you admit your mistakes, you are more able to connect with others on a deeper level. And you earn their respect because they learn they can trust you. They will be able to see that your strength comes from the inside, not the outside, because you are not trying to impress others with a false sense of perfection.

Humility is often viewed as a weakness. When I spoke at UCLA with Les Brown and Nick Vujicic in 2019, I decided to sit in the back of the room, in the audience, instead of on the platform with the other speakers. I wanted to get to know the audience, and by sitting among them, I met some great people! They had no idea I was going to speak later. Everyone was extremely nice, except one lady who was quite rude for no apparent reason. Regardless, I let it go. When it was my time to go up and speak, she tried to stop me from walking up front, not realizing I was a guest speaker. After my talk, she walked over to me, profusely apologizing for her behavior. She said she had no idea I was a speaker, and she attempted to give many reasons as to why she was rude. I told her not to worry, it was no big deal. Truly, I didn't hold it against her.

On another occasion, when I was consulting a credit union, I noticed that one of the customer representatives had the best attitude in the organization. The president of the credit union hired me to improve their customer service and marketing.

Later, I came to find out that the customer service representative was working as a cashier at a Popeyes. The CEO was very impressed with her positive attitude and her humility. Once, she made a mistake while ringing up his order and apologized to him, admitting the mistake and correcting it. He was so impressed on how she handled the situation that he offered her a job at the credit union. Many people would rather not admit if they made a mistake, but when you do, you will realize that humility truly is a virtue that leads to greater fortune. The customer service representative was eventually promoted to branch manager.

#4

DON'T STOP LOVING BIG

My younger self could have given up many times over. But through it all, I kept another lesson from my grandmother close to me. Love big. In fact, keep loving, especially when it is most difficult to do so.

Love is a choice, and we tend to be conditional with our love. Maybe we love only if our friends or family meet certain standards. I have seen over the years countless examples of marriages ending because one spouse or the other failed to live up to a certain ideal.

One day, my then twenty-three-year-old son was leaving with a cake in his hands.

I asked him, "Where are you going with that cake?"

He said that there was a ninety-nine-year-old lady who lived at the nursing home where he plays the piano to entertain them. Her family hadn't visited in years, and it was her birthday.

He chose to love big.

I've found the following steps helpful when striving to find the love within yourself . . . even during the most difficult times:

1. **Take it easy.**

    Do not stress yourself out trying to be perfect. Be the best you can be now, and do not try to solve the world's problems alone or all at one time. When you learn to take it easy and stress less, you focus less on your own problems and are able to see the beauty that surrounds you and the good qualities in other people. And while you're at it, stop demanding perfection from others. Loving is messy! Life does not have to be perfect to be fulfilling. Yes, we live in an imperfect world, one that can be ugly, painful, and miserable. But, out of life's adversities, we can learn to see the beauty in it all. Instead of looking at the thorns in the rosebushes, look at the beauty in the roses.

2. **Take the time to learn about the people in your life.**

    In one of my jobs, I became friends with a mailroom employee who dropped off our mail at our desks.

    One day the senior vice president of my department told me, "We don't talk to the help. You are in management, and you only associate with management."

    I was shocked and disheartened.

    I said, "If you took the time to get to know everyone in the company, you might learn something new. Did you know the mailroom employee is a famed blues guitarist who played with Etta James? Did you know he can play the guitar with his feet? His name is Curley Mays. He works here because he is retired and enjoys people. He'd rather be here than at home alone."

I gave my boss a copy of the CD that Curley Mays had given me. From that day on, the SVP treated Curley with the respect he, and everyone, deserves.

3. **At the start of each day, choose to be joyful, even during times of despair.**

Studies have found that you can trick your mind into being happy by smiling. So, even if you don't feel like smiling, smile anyway—you will be much more joyful.[4] Try it! It really works. A smile can infect a whole room. A smile can convey understanding, empathy . . . love.

4. **Relearn true communication.**

Communication begins with listening. Listen to others' points of view and identify ways to provide your own point of view in a civil manner. I have never before witnessed our society as divisive as it is today. I spent a lot of my childhood days at my grandma's beauty salon and grandpa's barbershop, which were located next to each other. I recall my grandfather talking politics with the patrons and sharing opposing points of view. Not once did anyone lose respect for one another, and they were able to share why they held their positions in a passionate yet civil manner.

Today, in many instances, if you hold an opposing political view, you are attacked verbally and sometimes physically! I have a friend who holds the opposite political view as me. We are able to discuss our views civilly and with respect. However, if we are in a social environment, we are often not able to share our views because we find people are not willing to listen. If you don't agree with their viewpoint, they don't want to hear you and feel you don't deserve the opportunity to freely share your thoughts.

Loving big means imagining yourself in the shoes of the other, and we seem to have forgotten this. We have stopped truly listening to others. And, because we've stopped listening and communicating, we have forgotten that it is okay to disagree. We can still make a concerted effort to agree to disagree. To listen to opposing views, while realizing that an opposing view should not stop the friendship or the love you have for friends and family. When communicating, listen to the other person, without resorting to personal attacks. And, if you are attacked, gently move the conversation back to the topic, or recognize that it may be time to "fold 'em" if the conversation is turning toxic. If your friends or family are unable to remain civil, it may be time to limit the time you spend with them.

#5

BECOME A MIRACLE.

My good friend Nick Vujicic, who was the main speaker for our inaugural GREATER event in Texas, said, "If you can't get a miracle, become one." Life is hard, it's challenging, and it comes with a ton of adversities. Some of us experience more adversities than others, but that is what makes life great. The hardness of life makes the triumphant moments even more glorious when we overcome.

Sometimes we expect miracles, even when we don't deserve them. Or, we expect a miracle by breaking natural law. Our world revolves around laws, but I'm referring to natural laws, not those created through legislation. For example, if you jump off a twelve-story building, gravity is going to propel you down to ground level. Yes, God is capable of carrying you back up to the building and saving you. However, rarely does God break natural law. Of course, this does not mean He can't, but He is not our personal genie or a personal God of our own making. If we decide to do something stupid, out of our own free will, and leap from a twelve-story building, we are going to face the consequences of our actions and die, or barely survive. If we decide to eat sugary foods every day and refuse to exercise or eat anything nutritious, we are going to experience the results of our diet with bad health. No, we won't grow muscles, we won't have energy, and our health will decline.

One of my favorite quotes from the movie *A Hidden Life* is, "If God gives us free will, we are responsible for what we do, or what we fail to do."

Nick Vujicic was born without arms and legs. No one knows why. He was bullied as a child. He didn't receive the miracle of arms and legs he prayed for. Instead, he decided to become a miracle. Today, he inspires millions of people worldwide with his inspirational speeches. Countless lives have been changed because of the work he has chosen to do: to bring hope into the hearts and minds of many.

Another friend of mine, Dr. Motte of Saudi Arabia, has impacted over 65,000 children in her country. Her motivation? She saw Nick Vujicic speak on YouTube. She said, "If he can impact many and he has no arms and legs, what's my excuse?" Dr. Motte is paying it forward.

You, too, can take your skills, gifts, talents, and knowledge—including your perceived weaknesses—and use them to become a miracle for someone else. If you choose to do so, your life will be richly blessed and your reward will be greater than anything in your wildest imagination.

Today, Nick has the most beautiful wife and four beautiful children. He is a blessed man.

How to be a miracle for someone else:

1. **Offer a word of encouragement.**

   When my friend Dr. Martin was there for me when I was fired, he was that miracle that pulled me out of my despair. Without his inspiration, I may not have climbed out of the emotional pit to reach GREATER heights!

2. **Gift items you no longer use.**

   It may seem like a simple thing, but you may be surprised how a simple gesture could be a miracle to someone else. I bought a bottle of wine at a wine castle when I was in Spain. I never used it; I just kept it in a dark place, as I had been told. They said the longer I kept it, the better it aged—and, as it turned out, increased in value. Since I never opened the bottle, I decided to give it to a couple for their New Year's celebration. They didn't drink wine, but they sure did need the money. (They are not the type of people who would ask for money or let you know they are in need.) They sold it to a neighbor who was a wine enthusiast and discovered that it was quite valuable. The couple to whom I gave the wine experienced a miracle: they had no idea how they were going to come across the extra money they needed at the time.

3. **Use what you have.**
   Start using your gifts, talents, and knowledge today! The next product, service, or business idea you bring to your boss may be the miracle people need to make the world a better place.

#6

LESSONS I LEARNED THROUGH GREATER

I'm always learning! With the new series of GREATER events, I have learned many new lessons that I will share with you.

1. **ALWAYS Have Your Lawyer Review Your Contracts**
   When the arena sent me the contract, I was so excited that I signed it immediately. With acts such as Jennifer Lopez and Styx performing at the arena, I thought, "If their contract is good enough for them, surely it's good enough for

me." I learned the hard way—through a huge financial loss and a huge chastising from my lawyer—to carefully read the fine print. Although we had a full house, we still lost money. I sent the contract to my lawyer, and he was shocked I had signed a contract without his review—something I had not done in the twelve years of working with him. Unfortunately, it was a binding contract that allowed no recourse.

2. **ALWAYS Know the Backgrounds of Those Who Surround You!**

A VIP guest presented himself as one of the "top speakers" to some of the administration staff at the school and asked the administration for permission to speak. He was not on the roster to speak, and none of us had ever heard him before. However, he insisted on speaking, and the administration thought it was great that he offered to do it for free, especially since he presented himself as a "professional speaker." Needless to say, no one could understand a word the speaker said. It was so quiet, you could hear the proverbial pin drop. Fortunately, the master of ceremonies quickly intervened and removed him peacefully from the stage.

3. **Don't Assume Famous People Have Integrity**

One of the scheduled speakers was removed from the roster because he was making racist comments against other groups of people. Often, we tend to place more value on someone because of seemingly impressive titles, money, or fame. We are all human. We all bleed red. There is no one who is above you or below you in value. Learn to look at people's actions, not their titles or the size of their bank accounts.

However, I choose to look at the lessons from the experiences I shared above. I now know how to choose who to work with. I learned to seek the advice of my attorney for all contracts. And, most importantly, I do not allow my mistakes to pull me down emotionally or spiritually—but to accept my mistakes as a learning opportunity for the future.

4. **Take Responsibility**

Despite the mistakes you make, the choice to make a change is yours—you just need to choose.

I remember the advice my grandparents gave me whenever I offered up a complaint, burden, or bad choice I had made.

My grandmother would ask, "Do share your burdens with me because you want me to share them with others, or do you share them because you are going to also share what you learned from this? Or are you about to share with me what you will do about it?"

Her questions slowed me down and had me question exactly why I was sharing this with her, and brought me to the following lessons:

I had to change my perspective.

I had to change my attitude.

I had to change my complaining.

I had to change my negative mindset.

I had to change my selfishness.
I had to change my bitterness.
I had to change my anger.
I had to change feeling sorry for myself.
I needed a new, restored heart, and to do that:
I chose to look for the blessing.
I chose to look for the beauty.
I chose to look for the small wins.
I chose to have a cheerful heart.
I chose to be loving and kind.
I chose to be accountable.
I chose to do the work.

CONCLUSION

The reality is that we could all come up with excuses of why we should fail because we live in a world where both good and evil exist, and that evil impacts all of us. But focusing on all the evil of the world and all the injustices we face only brings misery upon ourselves and those around us. There is also a lot of good in this world. And, as I mentioned earlier, life does not have to be perfect to be beautiful. I learned to look at how much I was loved by my grandmother and my mother, loved so greatly that they gave me a chance at life despite the obstacles. I learned to look at the beauty in the world amid the adversity. When I was in an abusive relationship and had to leave for the protection of my children, I learned to look at the beauty that the horrible, painful, and miserable marriage had produced—the beauty that was my children. I thank God every day for the gift He gave me of having talented children who bring so much joy to my life and to those around them: they are truly my GREATER FORTUNE!

ACKNOWLEDGMENTS

An expression of special thanks to:

My agent: Frank Weimann. Thank you for believing in the me, the underdog. I truly appreciate your support and encouragement to get this book published.

My publisher: BenBella Books. And all those at BenBella who contributed to this book, including the design, marketing, production, and publishing of this book: Alexa Stevenson, Jennifer Canzoneri, Kathleen Hollister, Adrienne Lang, Sarah Avinger, Leah Wilson, Monica Lowry, Rachel Phares, and Glenn Yeffeth.

My editors: Wes Smith, Joe Rhatigan, and Stephen Lang. Thank you for making my manuscript easier to read and fixing all of my grammatical errors.

The wonderful people in my life: Dr. William R. Martin, MD, and Rosie Martin, who have always believed in me, even when I didn't believe in myself. Deep Laxmi, you always provide encouragement and support through good times and rough times. Dr. Richard Gans, Dr. Frank Scarpino, Dr. Salvatore Gruttadauria, Christine Burks, and Noah Garten, thank you for your support in business. I could not do it without you. Mark Mackie, thank you for always being there for me throughout the years; you are the best attorney (probably one of the few honest ones left) and a great friend.

The inspirational people in my life: Thank you Nick Vujicic for telling me, "You need to write a book!" and introducing me to those who helped make it happen! Les Brown, thank you for believing in me, and driving several hours to my office in order to meet me in person the first time we met. You encouraged me to share how God has worked in my life with others by speaking and sharing the stage with you.

ABOUT THE AUTHOR

Twelve years ago, **Marie Cosgrove** was a single mother of four children when she was fired from balanceback™ because she "made too much" in commissions. Instead of becoming bitter, vengeful, and angry, she started her own company developing a different product. Two years after she was fired, she bought balanceback, the company that fired her. Skeptics and competitors said she would bankrupt the company and herself within six months. Nearly a decade later, balanceback is the world's leader in fall prevention, concussions, and brain and balance disorder diagnostic and treatment devices for clients including Dartmouth, Yale, Vanderbilt, University of Miami, VA hospitals, and Air Force bases nationally, as well as major hospitals and universities worldwide.

NOTES

Chapter One

1. Krucoff, Mitchell W., Suzanne W. Crater, Cindy L. Green, Arthur C. Maas, Jon E. Seskevich, James D. Lane, Karen A. Loeffler, Kenneth Morris, Thomas M. Bashore, and Harold G. Koenig. "Integrative Noetic Therapies as Adjuncts to Percutaneous Intervention during Unstable Coronary Syndromes: Monitoring and Actualization of Noetic Training (MANTRA) Feasibility Pilot." *American Heart Journal* 142, no. 5 (November 2001): 760–69. https://doi.org/10.1067/mhj.2001.119138.
2. Olver, Ian N., and Andrew Dutney. "A Randomized, Blinded Study of the Impact of Intercessory Prayer on Spiritual Well-Being in Patients With Cancer." *Alternative Therapies in Health & Medicine* 18, no. 5 (September 1, 2012): 18–27.

Chapter Three

1. Taelman, J, S Vandeput, A Spaepen, and S Van Huffel. "Influence of Mental Stress on Heart Rate and Heart Rate Variability." *Sprinter-Verlag Berlin Heidelberg* 22 (2008): 1366–69.

2. 12 Foundation, CK. "Homeostasis and Regulation in the Human Body." OpenCurriculum, 2019. https://opencurriculum.org/5385/homeostasis-and-regulation-in-the-human-body/.

3. Salleh, Mohd Razali. "Life Event, Stress and Illness." *Malays J Med Sci.* 4 (October 2008): 9–19.

4. "Rocky." *New York Times.* November 1, 1976. https://archive.nytimes.com/www.nytimes.com/packages/html/movies/best pictures/rocky-ar.html.

5. Tolbert, Kathryn. "An elusive musical gift could be at children's fingertips." The Free Library, accessed January 24, 2020, https://www.thefreelibrary.com/An+elusive+musical+gift+could+be+at+childrenAAEs fingertips.-a0205683588.

Chapter Four

1. "Social Security History." Social Security. 2019. https://www.ssa.gov/history/ottob.html.

2. Nikolov, Plamen, and Alan Adelman. "Short-Run Health Consequences of Retirement and Pension Benefits: Evidence from China." *SSRN Electronic Journal*, 2018. https://doi.org/10.2139/ssrn.3434626.

3. Binghamton University. "Early retirement can accelerate cognitive decline." ScienceDaily. www.sciencedaily.com/releases/2019/10/191029131506.htm (accessed January 25, 2020).

4. Smith, Beverley Jean. "A sleep and a forgetting: William Osler's beliefs about aging and death." Canadian Family Physician (Le Médecine de famille canadien) vol. 61, 2 (2015): 167–68.

Chapter Five

1. Walchover, Natalie. "What If Humans Had Eagle Vision?" LiveScience. Purch, February 24, 2012. https://www.livescience.com/18658-humans-eagle-vision.html.

Chapter Six

1. "Why Is It so Easy to Hold a Grudge?" Mayo Foundation for Medical Education and Research. November 4, 2017. https://www.mayoclinic.org/healthy-lifestyle/adult-health/in-depth/forgiveness/art-20047692.

2. Baykōse, Nazmi, Filiz Sahin, Ahmet Sahin, and Mehmet Emre Eryücel. "Is Self Talk of Athletes One of the Determinants of Their Continuous Sportive Confidence Level?" *Journal of Education and Training Studies*, 2, 7, no. 2 (January 28, 2019): 192. https://doi.org/10.11114/jets.v7i2.3999.

3. Turner, M.J., L Kirkham, and A.G. Wood. "Teeing up for Success: The Effects of Rational and Irrational Self-Talk on the Putting Performance of Amateur Golfers." *Psychology of Sport & Exercise* 38 (June 28, 2018): 148–53. https://www.sciencedirect.com/science/article/abs/pii/S1469029218301213

4. Cohen, Sheldon, Denise Janicki-Deverts, Ronald B. Turner, and William J. Doyle. "Does Hugging Provide Stress-Buffering Social Support? A Study of Susceptibility to Upper Respiratory Infection and Illness." SAGE Journals. 2014. https://journals.sagepub.com/doi/abs/10.1177/0956797614559284.

5. "Gallup 2019 Global Emotions Report." Gallup, Inc. 2019. https://www.gallup.com/analytics/248906/gallup-global-emotions-report-2019.aspx.

Chapter Seven

1. Mondics, Chris. 2011. "Elderly N.J. Patient's Last Years a Tale of Financial Fraud." *Philadelphia Inquirer*. April 17, 2011. https://www.inquirer.com/philly/business/20110417_Elderly_N_J__patient_s_last_years_a_tale_of_financial_fraud.html.

2. Stark, Tobias, Andrea Flache, and René Veenstra. (2013). "Generalization of Positive and Negative Attitudes Toward Individuals

to Outgroup Attitudes." Personality & social psychology bulletin. 39. 10.1177/0146167213480890.

3. University of Chicago Press Journals. "Negativity Is Contagious." ScienceDaily, October 7, 2007. http://www.sciencedaily.com /releases/2007/10/071004135757.htm.

4. Fowler, James H., and Nicholas A. Christakis. "Dynamic spread of happiness in a large social network: longitudinal analysis over 20 years in the Framingham Heart Study." *BMJ*. 2008 Dec 4; 337:a2338. doi: 10.1136/bmj.a2338. PMID: 19056788; PMCID: PMC2600606.

Chapter Eight

1. Hansson, B. "Company-based determinants of training and the impact of training on company performance; results from an international HRM survey." *Personnel Review*, vol. 36, no. 2 (2007): 311–31.

2. Bassi, I., J. Ludgwing, D. McMurer, and M. van Murer. "Profiting from learning firm-level effects of training investments and market implications." *Singaport Management Review*, vol. 24, no. 3 (2002): 61–76.

3. Schmidt, S. W. "The relationship between satisfaction with workplace training and overall job satisfaction." *Human Resource Development Quarterly*, vol. 18, no. 4 (2007): 481–98.

4. Bartel, A. "Measuring the employer's return on investments in training: Evidence from the literature." *Industrial Relations*, vol. 39, no. 3 (2000): 502–24.

5. Holzer, H., R. Block, M. Cheatham, and J. Knott. "Are training subsidies for firms effective? The Michigan experience." *Industrial and Labor Relations Review*, vol. 46, no. 4 (1993): 625–36.

6. Payne, S.C., and A.H. Huffman. "A longitudinal examination of the influence of mentoring on organizational commitment and turnover." *Academy of Management Journal*, 48 (2005): 158–68.

Chapter Nine

1. Gans, Richard R. "VNG Device Trial." Dizziness Testing. American Institute of Balance, 2006. http://dizzinesstest.com/vng-device -trial/.
2. Audiology, American Academy. "The Role of Videonystagmography (VNG)." *Audiology*, May 14, 2014. https://www.audiology.org /news/role-videonystagmography-vng.
3. Dutta, Sumedha, and Puja Khatri. "Servant leadership and positive organizational behaviour: The road ahead to reduce employees' turnover intentions." *On the Horizon* 25, no. 1 (2017): 60–82. https://doi.org/10.1108/oth-06-2016-0029.
4. University of Tennessee at Knoxville. "Psychologists find smiling really can make people happier." ScienceDaily. www.sciencedaily .com/releases/2019/04/190412094728.htm (accessed January 23, 2020).